PRAISE FOR THE BOOK

'Sudha's book, a compelling collection of letters from parents, eminent people whom we all admire and respect, gives us the chance to understand and share the secrets that these leaders learnt from their own parents. It is a book that each one of us should read and encourage others to read too'—Naina Lal Kidwai, Country Head, HSBC India, and President, FICCI

'An excellent compilation of letters, Sudha's book probably contains everything that any parent would want to tell their daughters'—Anand G. Mahindra, Chairman and Managing Director, Mahindra & Mahindra Ltd

'A delightful book on real life stories of the strong and emotional 'umbilical' cord between daughters and mothers/fathers!'—Kalpana Morparia, Chief Executive Officer, J.P. Morgan, India

'*Legacy* is a warm collection of thoughts, to make life worthwhile. In these times of scribbled post-its and illegible text messages, it was indeed a pleasure to come across these finely crafted letters'—Anu Aga, former Chairperson of Thermax Ltd and Member of Parliament

'An epic edition to be read, to be shared, to motivate, to remind, and to build a strong mind, heart, and character to succeed. Never has a book like this been written and one could only have hoped and expected it to be written and compiled by someone as insightful, warm, and incisive as Ms Menon'—Devita R. Saraf, CEO, Vu Technologies

'*Legacy* lays particular stress on values which are fast vanishing—to live with self-respect, dignity, having faith in a higher force, and to simply differentiate between right and wrong'—Amrita Patel, Chairperson, National Dairy Development Board and Foundation for Ecological Security

'Sudha's achievement has been that the book conveys the journey of both the parent and the daughter simultaneously, thus traversing time. I could see a busy but caring mother in Zia, a steady father in Padukone, and a sensitive parent in Narayana Murthy'—Meeran Chadha Borwankar, Additional Director General of Police (Prisons)

'I love the idea of the book—reminds me of my father and the weekly letters he used to send me while I was in college!'—Priya Paul, Chairperson, The Park Hotels

'A bold and fascinating concept'—Jerry Rao, founder and former CEO, Mphasis

Legacy

Letters from eminent parents to their daughters

Sudha Menon

EBURY
PRESS

An imprint of Penguin Random House

EBURY PRESS

USA | Canada | UK | Ireland | Australia
New Zealand | India | South Africa | China | Singapore

Ebury Press is part of the Penguin Random House group of companies
whose addresses can be found at global.penguinrandomhouse.com

Published by Penguin Random House India Pvt. Ltd
4th Floor, Capital Tower 1, MG Road,
Gurugram 122 002, Haryana, India

Penguin
Random House
India

First published in hardback by Random House India 2013
This paperback edition published 2015

Copyright © Sudha Menon 2013

ISBN 9788184007268

The views and opinions expressed in this book are the author's own and the
facts are as reported by her which have been verified to the extent possible, and
the publishers are not in any way liable for the same.

Typeset in GoudyOlSt BT by R. Ajith Kumar

Printed at Repro India Limited

www.penguin.co.in

MIX
Paper from
responsible sources
FSC® C047271

This is a legitimate digitally printed version of the book and therefore might not
have certain extra finishing on the cover.

To my parents,
my conscience keepers,
without whom my world would have been
a different place.
I love you, forever.

CONTENTS

CONTENTS

FOREWORD

Sudha's book, a collection of letters from inspirational men and women, is a reiteration of my belief that our parents can be our best teachers—mine certainly have been for me and my two brothers. It is from our parents that we internalize the values that shape our lives.

N.R. Narayana Murthy's letter to his daughter Akshata is a delight to read—he comes across as a doting father who is keen that his daughter benefits from the wealth of his own experience. I love the way he tells her to talk to her own daughters about their ancestors and their great accomplishments. It is heart-warming to read his thoughts about the struggles of women at work and how he is inspired by them.

Only a truly global leader like Narayana Murthy can tell his daughter to become a citizen of the world in every sense while simultaneously asking her to be a proud Indian, wherever in the world she lives.

Looking back at my own life after all these years, I can say without hesitation that I was lucky to have been born to my parents, the two extraordinary individuals who shaped my life and made me what I am today. I owe them everything that I have achieved.

Although my father is no more, he remains my strongest source of inspiration. Through my letter to my parents, I hope to convey what they mean to me.

Dearest Daddy and Mummy,

When you told me to consider brewing as a profession decades ago, it was rare for a girl to go out and even get a job for herself. All she was expected to do was complete her education and wait for a suitable man to come along so that she could get married and settle down.

Daddy, you were not the one to tread the beaten path— nor would you let your children do so. You made sure that your only daughter was no different from your two sons. After graduating in Zoology, I was wondering what I could do with my life when you completely stumped me one day by asking me to consider brewing as a profession. Being in the brewery business, you knew it had great potential in India and that I could apply my college education to my career.

Being your daughter, I soon found myself in Australia, studying to be a brewmaster—a profession that, even in a developed country like Australia, was a man's world. It was challenging but also fun being the lone girl in a room full of men who possibly thought I was out of my mind to be in that class! That was the turning point of my life, in many ways. On my return to India, I went from brewery to brewery in pursuit of employment but soon realized that the brewing world in India was not ready for a lady brewer. This was the first time I faced failure but strangely, it made me even more determined to succeed, I might never have become an entrepreneur. Biocon would never have been born but for the fact that I refused to let somebody else's prejudices dictate my life.

It was your faith in me, Daddy, that I would do something worthwhile with my education that laid the foundation of my own belief in myself. You were the one who showed me that gender has nothing to do with one's dreams. You often said to me: 'If you are intelligent and willing to work hard, you can make anything out of your life.' It was these seeds of wisdom that led me to apply my knowledge of fermentation to develop and pioneer a biotechnology-led enzymes business in India.

You also said that knowledge knows no gender divide. I know it is true today. It is completely possible to bridge the gender divide by being strong-willed, which is what I was as a young woman starting out on a singularly lonely journey into entrepreneurship. I continue to be strong-willed, heading an enterprise whose nucleus is the power of imagination and innovation—which is how I was able to transform my enzymes business into a fully-integrated biopharmaceuticals enterprise that it is today. Fermentation Science, a programme that I started with when I was studying to be a brewer, still remains at the core of our business expertize today.

I am self-assured and strong-willed thanks to the support from you and Mummy—and because you taught me to believe in myself. Had you not treated me as equal to my brothers, I may have suffered an inferiority complex being a woman and even diffident. This is what still happens in many Indian households where young women often grow up feeling they are not good enough—and it is a real pity that they were not blessed with enlightened parents like you.

The most fundamental truth that I learnt from you, Daddy, was this: you have to earn your right over anything you want. I dreamt of studying medicine as a young girl but was so arrogant about my abilities that I applied for admissions to just one college, St. John's in Bangalore. When the results were declared, I found to my horror that my name was not on the list of those admitted to the college. The only option then was to pay a hefty capitation fee for admission to a private college that offered medical education.

I turned to you then but my heart broke when you simply said 'No'! I wept and ranted and accused you of being unfair to me because I was a girl child. Today, I am grateful that you stuck to your guns and told me that you would never spend a single rupee on capitation fee, as a matter of principle. You told me in no uncertain terms: 'If you want something, work for it. Don't buy your way through things because, if you do, you will never respect yourself.' Years later, my admiration for your strength of character continues to grow—especially in the context of the challenges of growing corruption this country faces today—as does my appreciation for the value of what you were trying to teach me. To this day I am proud of the fact that I have never 'bought' any favour or paid a bribe to facilitate anything that I needed. I simply work till I get to my goal. Thank you, Daddy.

While I shared a deep bond with Daddy, I am deeply inspired by you Mummy. You grew up in Gujarat in a traditional family that placed a high premium on educating seven daughters and their only son. The difference, however, was that they did not think their daughters needed a career. When you married Daddy, you did so understanding that you would spend your life being a housewife and raising kids. But Mummy, you did that with such joy and commitment! Despite your traditional background, you raised us differently, exposing us to your work at the Catholic mission that you volunteered with every week. You encouraged us to interact with your friends from different nationalities, religions, and backgrounds. This instilled a healthy worldview in all of us—that diversity is good and that we must respect different people and their various points of view. And that there is space on this earth for everyone and everything—a lesson that stands us in good stead even today.

Most importantly, Mummy, from you I learnt courage and determination. When Daddy passed away, you were devastated and bereft. You had lost the one person who was your anchor and for a while, it seemed as if you felt your life was over. And then, you surprised us all by emerging from the depths of your grief and despondence to set up your own automated laundry service and you called it 'Jeeves' after your favourite P.G. Wodehouse character. You are one of the bravest and most resourceful women I have known—and I am proud to be your daughter.

I look upon all young Indian girls who are approaching adulthood with a mix of anxiety and intrepidation as to what the future holds and reflect on my own youth when I stood at similar crossroads. I would like to say to them: We woman are equal citizens of this country. A good education and pursuit of a career or vocation that is useful to society is what really matters. Making money is not everything; adding value to society with impactful work is.

I would also like to tell them—as I have learnt from you, Daddy and Mummy—there are no shortcuts in life. There will be successes and failures, pain and gain, and there will always be plenty of sceptics, critics, and people with prejudice—as I have learnt through all these years of building Biocon. Life's rich tapestry is made of all of these. Your task is simply to take everything in your stride and forge ahead. We women are a resilient lot; we are able to take failure and other setbacks in our stride.

My message to all the young girls in our country is that sometimes your weakness can be your biggest strength, and like the handicap in golf, your weakness can be your biggest advantage. If indecisiveness and diffidence are your perceived weaknesses, work quietly on converting these into unwavering self-confidence and decisiveness, and then, go out and conquer the world.

With my deepest love,
Your daughter,
Kiran

Kiran Mazumdar-Shaw
CMD, Biocon Ltd
Bangalore, 2013

Ajay Piramal

Ajay Piramal is a man of many interests. An animal lover, wildlife photographer, and a whimsical writer, Piramal is also the man who almost single-handedly charted one of corporate India's most lucrative deals when he sold Piramal Healthcare's domestic formulations business to the US-based Abbott Labs for a stunning US$ 3.7 billion in 2010, catapulting him into the league of the country's top 50 billionaires.

It is easy to get intimidated by his reputation and by the stillness of his top floor office at Piramal Towers in central Mumbai, where priceless art and verses from ancient scriptures, engraved in granite, compete for space.

The man himself is disarmingly humble and down-to-earth. Though he initially had to be persuaded to speak about his life, once he got talking, there was no stopping him. His tales were so enthralling that I went back not once but three times, to know the real person behind the veneer of his public persona.

At the age of 29, Piramal found himself at the crossroads of life, shouldering the responsibility of managing a flagging textiles business while ensuring the well-being of his own family and that of his brother who tragically passed away after suffering from cancer, leaving behind a young widow and two little children.

Many in the industry predicted that the business would not survive owing to his lack of experience, but the relatively 'inexperienced' Piramal took the challenge head-on and the last few decades, has seen it grow into a formidable US$ 2 billion conglomerate with presence in manufacturing, pharmaceuticals, real estate, finance, and telecom.

The astute businessman lives his life and manages his business drawing inspiration from the Bhagavad Gita. He quotes extensively from it, which is not surprising considering the fact that every weekend, he and his wife attend a class on the teachings of the dharmic scriptures conducted by his guru.

A great believer in the power of sharing one's privileges, his philanthropic enterprise, The Ajay G. Piramal Foundation runs multiple programmes for the rural poor in his home state of Rajasthan. He is also the Chairman of Pratham India, India's largest non-governmental organization in the education sector, reaching out to over 33 million children through its 'Read India' campaign.

Piramal finds great inspiration in Rabindranath Tagore's words:

Let me not pray to be sheltered from dangers,
But to be fearless in facing them.

Let me not beg for the stilling of my pain,
But for the heart to conquer it.

Let me not look for allies in life's battlefield,
But to my own strength.

Let me not crave in anxious fear to be saved,
But hope for the patience to win my freedom.

Grant me that I may not be a coward,
Feeling your mercy in my success alone.

But let me find the grasp of your hand
In my failure.

Piramal's letter to his daughter Nandini, an executive director at the group's flagship company, Piramal Healthcare, gives a fascinating insight into his own journey to finding unbelievable success and mental bliss.

Dear Nandini,

A long time ago, when I was a young man of 24, my father, whom I was very close to, passed away unexpectedly, leaving the family without its anchor. He was the head of our family in every sense of the way. We depended on him for guidance and emotional sustenance and his death left us rudderless and the family business, without a leader. Somehow, we recouped with the help of your uncle, my brother Ashok, who became the new father figure in our lives and took over the family business. It was a difficult time. Soon after dad's demise, the family itself went through a difficult division of assets and I chose to remain with Ashok in the textile business which constituted 90 percent of our business interests while my other brother decided to move away.

On January 1, 1982, just days after the division, our business was hit by a trade union strike. This was the infamous Datta Samant textile strike that paralyzed Mumbai's thriving textile industry and our business went into limbo for the eighteen months that the strike lasted. Our valuations took a severe drubbing and while we were still coming to grips with the losses, my beloved brother, who was just 35 years of age at the time, was diagnosed with cancer. He suffered from the disease for over a year before passing away in 1984. I was 29-years-old then.

Suddenly, at 29, I found myself all alone, faced with the prospect of shouldering the responsibility of not just running the family business which was in shambles but also of being in charge of two families—mine and my brother's. He had left behind a young wife and three children, the youngest of who was merely 3-years-old. Life seemed like a huge burden, an impossible task, and there were a lot of people who wondered how I could handle all this since I was an inexperienced young man. They thought the business would fold up without a leader, in no time.

But it was my faith and the spiritual teachings of my father that carried me through this difficult phase. He had a great belief in God and in a superior force above, which he believed, watches us at all times. So even though the world thought I was inexperienced, I knew that both my father and my brother had complete faith and confidence in me and that helped instilling a self-belief.

Your mother, Swati, too was no different. She always gave me the support and strength to face challenges and had the ability to look at the brighter side of things, even in the most difficult of circumstances.

How else can you explain the fact that just a couple of months before my brother passed away, we acquired Gujarat Glass, a move into a completely uncharted territory for us? My brother and Swati encouraged me to follow up that acquisition even when he was seriously ill because they believed that it was important to diversify our business so we would not be vulnerable to factors over which we had no control. And so, even though we were steeped in debt at that point, we made the acquisition in order to de-risk ourselves. Twenty years later, our textile business constituted less than 5 percent of our total business. We had succeeded in completely changing the complexion of the group.

We made that acquisition in June and my brother passed away in August, leaving me with a crucial life lesson: Life has to go on, no matter how big the loss or how deep the suffering from life's unexpected surprises are.

Looking back now, I can see how lucky I was to have people in my life who had enough faith in me to let me make mistakes and grow from them. None of us can learn without making a few mistakes of our own.

I also learnt that what we look upon as really hopeless, bad times, are merely temporary phases which will also pass and life will be smooth again. I learnt courage from my brother who valiantly fought cancer, never giving up once or complaining about his lot in life. Never once did he say:

'Why me?' I learnt from him to always be optimistic. He also taught me that the difficult phases in life are moments in passing and that a situation that you think you will not be able to survive will not seem so bad when you look back at it. We as humans have the power to overcome our circumstances, all we need, is the courage to take firm decisions and stick to them.

That phase of my life also taught me other crucial life lessons which I have strived to follow over the years. I realized the importance of prioritizing things. I decided that my family came first, our health second, and work third. I learnt to love unconditionally and selflessly, without expecting anything in return. For me, the love that a mother has for her child is the purest form of love. Sadly, most of the times as parents, we go on to expect our children to give back to us in some form for the love we showered on them in their childhood. Love given in expectance of something in return is a transaction. You are a mother of a little daughter now and remember this as you raise her, Nandini.

Much as it may sound like a discourse, Nandini, there is great inner peace and joy to be gained from sacrificing for our loved ones. Both you and your husband have careers and aspirations of your own, which I am happy about. But let me caution you that if a marriage has to succeed, you will have to sacrifice more than your husband. And now that you are the mother of a child, you have a greater responsibility to shoulder and must have to sacrifice a little bit more than your husband. Believe me, giving is infinitely more satisfying than taking.

Dear Nandini, I want to remind you of your growing up years and of the support you found in your family in fulfilling all your dreams. When you expressed your desire to go abroad to pursue your undergraduate studies, we gladly sent you off because we believed in you. It was not an easy thing to do for us, though. Fifteen years ago, it was a big thing for a traditional Marwari girl to go out of the country to study, but we respected your need to do it. And when you returned after honing your skills at the Stanford Graduate School of Business, you got a place in the family business earned from your own merit.

You moved in to steer a significant portion of it. I must say you are doing a sterling job out of it. I believe in letting you learn from your own mistakes just as my father allowed me to do and I am hoping you will let your child explore this world on her own too.

But I want to tell you that while work has to be an important aspect of your life, what is also important is for you to strive to make a difference in the lives of the people around you with the work that you do. I cannot emphasize the virtue of giving back to the society which made you who you are.

Nandini, life will have its ups and downs. Suffering is a part of life, but how you face those adversities is what will set you apart from the rest. Strive to tackle your challenges, the hurdles in your life, with equanimity. It is this ability that will shape the person you become and determine the course that your life takes.

Believe in God because that is what will keep you on

the straight path. No matter what your situation in life is, ultimately you have to believe in a higher power who will sort things out for you in times of need. What helped me during the worst phases of my life was my very strong belief that whatever happens, happens for a reason. I really do believe that and surrender myself in the hands of God during such times. I truly believe that this also makes a person stronger and fearless.

I know that you're too young to understand most of this, but I am sure that faith and spirituality will come to you as the years pass by and you have seen life the way I have. Faith takes time, but I am confident it will grow as you mature.

But even if you don't have as much faith right now, I am glad to see what a high level of integrity and morals you subscribe to, sometimes more than I have been able to adopt myself. You see life in black and white while I am able to see the shades of grey that life's countless situations bring.

I am glad you are inherently a good human being, someone who will not intentionally harm anyone and someone who will not do something if she is not convinced whether it is the right thing to do.

As you go along the journey of life, I can't underline enough for you the value of nurturing compassion as a virtue. Have compassion towards the people around you and don't judge them at face value—there are so many reasons behind why people behave the way they do or become who they are. Who are we to judge them?

I believe, too, that each of us has to have the courage to do what we think is right at each stage of our life.

I have always believed in the power of gratitude. Dear Nandini, I want you to be grateful for everything God has given you. A grateful person is a happy person. I am grateful for what my God, my family, my children, and my friends do for me. I have experienced the peace that comes from being grateful. Gratitude also makes us humble. Nandini, you have a lot of things—great wealth, great education—so you have every reason not to be humble. It is important to remember, then, to be grateful and humble and also to remember that there is a reason why you were born in this family. You could be one of the hundred thousand others in this city. Be grateful for the parents you have, your husband, your little child, for your family, and your friends. Gratitude and humility are virtues mentioned even in our scriptures which say that to be a true devotee, you have to be humble.

I know many of these things sound too idealistic—stuff that newspapers and books will often preach about—but these are the truths that help you along the way as a young wife, mother, professional, and a member of a larger community.

Often times I am asked about my own attitude towards wealth and what I taught my own children about it. I taught you that wealth is not something to be ashamed of or to keep away from. You are a trustee of the wealth given to you by your parents and by the Lord. Don't hoard your wealth. Instead, live the life you want with the wealth you have been blessed with, but also make it beneficial for the good of the larger community. Share your prosperity. That is what I learnt while growing up and that is what I am confident you *will do too. I am joyous when I see how involved you are in the various projects that we run in Rajasthan to provide good quality education, clean drinking water, healthcare, and employment for women.*

Nandini, I know how much you enjoy your work; but while following your career, also give your family more of yourself along the way. The role of a spouse is to bring balance to the relationship. It also means respect for your partner. I respect what your mother does and I have the self-confidence to take pride in her achievements. A marriage is not about proving to be better than your partner. If your husband's work takes him to another country, I would wish for you to follow him. Your child and your husband should take precedence in this phase of your life.

Now that you are a mother, I want to tell you about the power of sacrificing for your children. There is really no substitute for devoting time to your children. If you want to bring them up as good human beings, set an example for them by living the life that you want them to follow and, above all, loving them unconditionally. I have always lived my life keeping in mind one seminal principle: Do only those things that make my children proud of me and avoid the stuff that will make them hang their heads in shame. Gangsters and underworld dons wield enormous power and have loads of money but I can guarantee you, their children are not proud of them.

As a young man, I gave time to my family and I continue to do so today. You know I'm not too fond of partying and my best moments are the ones I spend in the company of my loved ones. Nandini, our time on this earth is limited, so learn to prioritize and organize your days in order to maximize that time. Twenty-four hours is sufficient time and if you organize things properly, there is a lot you can get done within this time. Technology has made it easier for a lot more to be achieved in the same number of hours. I am able to do so much more with my time today than I could, thirty years ago.

Nandini, as I grow older, what gives me immense joy is spending time with myself and introspecting.

I never think ahead. I believe that if you just keep on doing the right thing, the results of your labour will follow soon after. You cannot control the results, but you can control what you are doing. It is your actions that will determine the results.

Let me end with my favourite lines here. There is a reason why these have become my personal favourite and our corporate credo.

You are what your deep, driving desire is
As your desire is, so is your will
As your will is, so is your deed
As your deed is, so is your destiny
(Taken from the Brihadaranyaka Upanishad)

Love,
Papa

Amit Chandra

Amit Chandra, Managing Director of Bain Capital Advisors, a leading global private investment firm in India, hailed from a middle-class family which did not have any disposable income. But he is today involved in philanthropic activities, in a country where charity as a way of life is yet to catch on.

Chandra, one of corporate India's head honchos, tasted success at a relatively young age, heading DSP Merrill Lynch in his early thirties. And yet, he felt a void in his life that left him restless and unfulfilled. It was then that he turned to Vipassana, an ancient Buddhist form of meditation, to figure out what was missing.

When he emerged from the period of silence that Vipassana requires of its practitioners, he had the answer: he wanted to do more for the community around him and give back from the riches that he had gathered on the journey to the top echelons of corporate life. Chandra is today a patron and a member of the board of several of India's most effective and well-known NGOs, doing remarkable work in the field of education for the underprivileged and for children with special needs, such as The Akanksha Foundation schools in Mumbai and Pune, The Research Society for the Care, Treatment and Training of Children in Need of Special Care, the Jai Vakeel School for the Mentally Challenged,

Give India, the YMCA Boys' Home and Vocational Training Centre in Andheri, and the Tata Medical Centre and Cancer Patients Aid Association in Kolkata.

A young Chandra learnt the merit of sharing one's resources at a very young age from his mother who ran a very frugal household and gave her limited resources to the needy ones in their community. A family of academicians—his uncle was the head of the National Council for Educational Research and Training (NCERT) and his brother-in-law, Nitin Nohria, is currently the Dean of Harvard Business School—they also believed in sharing knowledge. Both he and his sister taught the domestic help in the family the basics of literacy from their childhood years.

Chandra is inspired by the story of Chuck Feeney, the American billionaire, also called the James Bond of philanthropy, who wrote away his untold wealth to aid a range of social initiatives. And Chandra walks the talk. A couple of years ago, he and his wife Archana, a willing partner to him in various social initiatives, wrote away the bulk of their vast personal wealth to various causes close to their heart.

'I believe that wealth is an incredible tool and a godsend blessing. When used productively, it can bring long-lasting joy and true happiness; but when misused, or accumulated without purpose, it can become a disease that destroys families and relationships.' Such Chandra writes in this bittersweet note to his daughter, Anika.

18

My dearest Anna,

I know that at the time of my writing this letter to you, you are too young to understand some of what I want to convey. But this is a letter that I want you to read when you are a young woman, when you start witnessing the uncertainties of life, facing the breadth of right and wrong, and start seeking meaning in some of it, defining the purpose of your own life in the process. I want to start by telling you that even though every child is special to her parents, you are more than special to us. You came to us, with the blessings of God, after your mother and I had almost given up the hope of ever having a child of our own. Every time your mother suffered a miscarriage, it was not just the emotional and physical pain that she went through that affected us, but more the thought that both us love children so much and therefore really wanted to have one of our own! You came to us in the eleventh year of our marriage, and I can't fully express how your coming into our lives has changed our world for the better.

Each day that you show me a new skill that you mastered, or tell me about something new that you learnt in some class, or share with us some experience you had with a friend, is an incredible feeling. At times I am amazed at how quickly you are growing, sometimes I just get lost in the joy or concern of your own experience, and often your experience takes me back to my own days as a little kid. Your wonderment at the simple things in life fills our lives with joy, and I hope and pray that this ability to keep life uncomplicated and enjoy happiness through simple things stays with you throughout.

Anna, you are just over 7-years-old but you don't know the impact you have already had on our family. Each one of us—your mother, your two grandmothers, and I—are touched by your unbound enthusiasm for things, your mischievous streak, your unquenchable curiosity, your sense of humour, and your somewhat calm nature. Someday, I hope to also learn from you the ability to be relatively more disciplined and dogged when not playing to one's strengths, skills that I have struggled to adopt in my everyday life! For example, your passion for gymnastics and the determination to do well at it amazes me. What you lack in a sportsperson's physique, thanks to your parents' genes, you make up with your determination and effort. Most people play to their strengths, probably taught to do so as kids. However, life is about facing many situations, and often one has to play to one's weakness, so this trait is truly a great asset to have. I have no doubt that determination is central to making things happen, even when faced with the biggest odds.

Anna, every parent wants the best for their children. However, the pushes and pulls of day-to-day life often prevent them from fully imparting the knowledge they have gained from a life filled with experiences. Writing this letter to you is therefore an incredible opportunity for me to think hard and pen everything that I have wanted to impart to you, to tell you what I think is important for you to know in the long run.

From my own experience, and from looking at people

around me, I have come to believe that life should be about two things —first, a quest for true happiness, and second, a journey to make a positive impact, both upon yourself, and the society at large. Often we end up confusing our objectives and chase things that we think will eventually get us one of these two, but in doing so, we lose track of the real objectives. We get obsessed with our jobs, in the pursuit of something material, certain relationships, or some challenging situation, as a result of which life gets into a rut, becomes very one-dimensional, or pushes one to despair. I can tell you, with confidence, that it is important to pause and frequently ask ourselves if we have either truly made ourselves happy, or done something positive for our loved ones, and more importantly, if we are contributing to somehow making the world a better place than what we see before us.

Dear Anna, I see that as a little girl you are already doing this in your own small way by being happy with simple things of life, and lighting up the lives of your parents and grandparents with the way you spread joy and affection. I hope and pray that you will continue to find ways to do so for the rest of your life. I am asked occasionally what my wishes are for you and I always say that what I really want for you is to be happy and spread happiness around. Everything else is secondary, for what's the use of success or wealth or fame if you are not at peace with yourself and not making a positive impact upon those around you?

Let me now tell you about what has shaped these beliefs and learning in my life. Anna, for the many years before you were born, I worked very hard and without any sense of balance. I have come to learn that lack of balance can lead to some form of success, but in a very one-dimensional manner, and unless appropriately balanced, it can be at the expense of long-term happiness. I was fortunate that before I was even 35-years-old , I was running nearly all of DSP Merrill Lynch, which at that time was India's leading investment bank, so fame and fortune came to me somewhat early in life. However, towards the end of my thirteenth year with the firm, I realized that despite having everything most would aspire for, there was something missing in my life.

I spent a long time trying to figure out what was missing in my life and took some time off to go to a Vipassana camp. Sometimes, the realization comes to you a little late because once you start leading your life a particular way, it's really tough to bring in significant changes. Vipassana helped me enormously. Honestly, I didn't learn the meditation technique at the camp, but the mandatory silence at the camp gave me eleven days with myself, helping me seek answers to the many questions I had about the purpose of my life and how I wanted to lead it.

I reflected then and continue to reflect now on what was missing, and I want to share with you what I have learnt. Firstly, Anna, while I gained a lot, I also paid a big price for that lack of balance in many parts of my life. If I was able to turn back the clock, I would lead a more balanced life, even if it would mean not having had the same degree of success or even if that success had taken longer to come. But I am convinced it would have been a more enjoyable, more durable journey in the long run.

Back home, with a clearer picture of the life I wanted, I decided to give up my job at DSP Merrill Lynch right at the peak of my career. I could have easily continued there or I could have gone on to manage a larger company, or earn more fame and fortune, but that wasn't all what I wanted to do. In fact, I figured that my job was taking away a lot of flexibility from what I really wanted to do with my life. I felt that I needed to course-correct my life, before it was too late in terms of choosing a new career that would be more intellectually stimulating, but would give me more flexibility with how I wanted to spend my time with myself, and on things outside the work place.

You mother understands the need for balance in life and I envy her ability to lead her life with a sense of balance. It is my hope that you will learn from my mistakes, and also inherit this ability from her so that you have a better life.

Dear Anna, please don't misunderstand what I am saying. While I fervently hope that you cultivate a sense of balance in life as early as possible, I hope that it does not happen at the cost of drive and intensity in your chosen calling. I just hope that while doing so, you will balance your career pursuits with your responsibility, to yourself from a health perspective or with your relationships, and to society more broadly.

Sometimes I look at your mother and feel envious of how she has struck what I feel is the right balance—one which works for her, for her family, and for the society at large. It is not easy working in the not-for-profit space. Your mother chose to work with an NGO that serves mentally challenged children. It is tough to be inspired to serve a section of society when you have never been impacted by the cause directly or indirectly. It is a struggle, but with some smart time management, flexi- timings, working from home, and leveraging the power of the cell phone, your mama makes sure that she does her best for this cause but is still always there for you and the family at every point. And while doing all this, she finds time for her exercise, meditation, and pranic healing practice, which she believes is critical to her own physical and spiritual well-being. Your mother does sometimes wonder if she is being productive to the best of her abilities, but doesn't fully appreciate how I love the balance she has found in her life.

I have also discovered that it is very important for any person not to live life being distracted or pushed by other people's opinions, influences, or expectations. In doing so, we land up doing things that don't really give us any lasting sense of joy, and because the passion is missing, we can't make any meaningful contribution to what we are doing. As children grow up, parents want them to be something that they themselves dreamt of becoming, or what they believe will be appreciated by others. For you, we don't want anything of that sort. Our dream for you is to seek the counsel of well-wishers, but follow your own dream, whatever that is, without the restrictions of parental or societal expectations.

When I was growing up, career choices were dictated by necessity. If anybody wanted to make a middle-class living they had to become an engineer, a doctor, or a chartered accountant. The relative good fortune that we've had, and *the evolution of our country, will give you some flexibility to do what you want to do. Whatever it is you choose to do, remember that you don't have to be rich or famous or successful, you just need to enjoy the journey and be happy. As you grow up, your mom and I are hoping that we are able to give you the full breadth of experiences in life so that you can discover what you really want to do.*

I was very lucky that, by God's grace, I landed up doing things that have really given me enjoyment, but at various points over the years, I could have actually got pushed into something because it was the right thing to do from a society or family point of view and I would have been miserable if I had actually gone down that path. Life sometimes presents you with these small left or right turns and you land up on a completely different road. I got very lucky in landing up doing something I wanted to do. But in your case, I want to make sure it's not serendipity but a more thoughtful process that arises from within you, so that you know what will give you joy. While we will counsel and debate with you, we are always going to be okay with any well-thought through choices that you might make. Yes, we will be as happy if you want to sing, or become a dancer, or serve a cause fulltime, as we will be if you want to become a chef and start a restaurant!

Darling Anna, I now want to share with you two other big lessons that I have learnt along the way, the first of which is that often people grossly overestimate the value of Intelligence Quotient and grossly underestimate the value of Emotional Quotient (terms that you will learn to appreciate as you grow). I have learnt that every parent pushes their child on the Intelligence Quotient aspect. Mostly this is marked by a desire for their child to be a topper. What I really want is to raise you in such a way that your emotional quotient and ability to think flourishes over simple academic excellence. I am convinced that in the long run, as a thinker, and a more emotionally balanced person, you will get a lot more out of life, than someone purely aspiring for straight 'A's!

The other learning that I want to share with you is that if there is one other thing that will truly distinguish you, it will be compassion. As you grow, you will begin to appreciate how important a quality this is, given the opportunity to spread happiness to those you know and the many others you do not, in this very unequal world we live in. Instead of lecturing you about being a good human being, we have and will continue to do our best to demonstrate to you through leading by example. From working with children, we know how incredibly observant kids are, and how much they absorb from simple observation. And so, my dear Anna, we hope you will learn compassion from the way we conduct ourselves at home, with each other, and with the domestic help who works with us.

We believe that compassion will also be kindled by the exposure that you will get to observe how to positively impact those less privileged, and then have the opportunity to practice this as you keep growing. This is why, when you were still a very little child, you celebrated some of your birthdays at the Asha Sadan orphanage. I don't know if you *still remember but last year you actually participated for the first time by serving the kids at the orphanage the goodies that we had taken along. You happily played with them and seemed to have a great time at the party. I know that you also enjoy giving biscuits to urchins at traffic lights, and have got to understand why that is a good idea and giving them money is not. Do you remember the time we went to the Sobo Central Mall for a little outing, and I bought you a giant lollipop that had totally bedazzled you? If you do, you will also remember how when we came out of the mall, a poor boy at entrance asked you for the lollipop. Initially, you were confused, but then when I nodded and smiled, you happily gave it away, and we trooped back in to buy you a new one. When we came back out, the little boy had come back with a friend, whose look begged you for the same generosity! It warmed my heart when you looked at me for approval and once again gave away your treat. I can still see how excited you were to see the boys so happy with their unexpected treat, and we went back in for you to receive a reward of two giant lollipops.*

My dear Anna, I now want to tell you about a subject that deeply engrosses me and one that I know you will also reflect on as you grow older—the purpose of wealth. I want you to know my views on this because it will also help you understand some of my own actions, which are somewhat counter to established practices of our times. I believe that wealth is an incredible tool and a godsend blessing. When used productively, it can bring long-lasting joy and true happiness, but when misused, or accumulated without purpose, it can become a disease that destroys families and relationships.

I want your pursuit for your passions to be driven more by your desire to excel and be happy, than the desire to simply earn wealth. True wealth is happiness, and in my own experience, true wealth will chase you if you do the right things. Don't be mistaken, my love, we certainly do not want you to be lazy. We certainly want you to explore your full potential, but with a sense of balance and not a mindless pursuit of wealth. Growing up in very affluent surroundings, my mother would never push us to study, but instead, she would explain to us that if we wanted to be successful, it would solely be on the basis of the values she sought to instil in us and our own effort to build our careers. It is up to you to make your destiny, she would say and your aunts and I took it to heart and never gave our parents any cause for complaint on this count. I can see that at a young age, you are already so conscientious with your work for the sake of learning.

Sometimes your mother and I worry that the level of affluence that you are born into, is very different from what we had, and could end up being a handicap for you instead of being your strength. That worry shapes a lot of decisions that your mother and I keep making, including the way we seek to live our lives a few notches below our monetary capability. It also shapes, among other factors, how we think about the concept of inheritance. We are very clear, Anna, that while ensuring your education and basic *comfort, we will use most of the wealth that god blesses us with, to drive various causes impacting the less privileged. This is why we have a very active program for making sure that we keep doing a lot with the wealth that's created, on an on-going basis though wonderful organizations like the Akanksha Foundation schools in Mumbai and Pune, The Research Society for the Care, Treatment and Training of Children in Need of Special Care, the Jai Vakeel School for the Mentally Challenged, GiveIndia, the YMCA Boys' Home and Vocational Training Centre in Andheri, and the Tata Medical Centre and Cancer Patients Aid Association in Kolkata.*

Giving as a way of life and a path to happiness is something we would wish for you to eventually adopt. I have seen too much conflict arising out of money. There is a sense of entitlement that arises among inheritors that often distorts their relationships with their parents and siblings and wrecks families. That wealth also creates the illusion that there is no need to push yourself since you know your parents have made enough for you. I've seen this in large business families, and even with friends.

The reason we want you to be a giving person is not because you will see it publicly acknowledged, but because you will feel that it's the right thing for you.

My dear Anna, I have said a lot, but I realize how small we all are in front of God's bigger picture and how little is really within our control. So, let me end by first thanking God for blessing me with you. I love you very dearly and everything I have said is because of that love which makes me want everything for you. I would like to bless you from the bottom of my heart with all my prayers, hope that you find true and lasting happiness in your life, and bring great joy to everyone around you.

With lots of love and best wishes,
Your Dada

Capt. Gopinath

It is hard not to be touched by Capt. Gopinath's restless, infectious energy, his seemingly endless optimism, and his sheer positivity.

Over my years as a business journalist, I have followed his life through the pages of newspapers, admired his courage and determination to tread where most men with an eye on the balance sheet would never dare step, and blessed him for making air travel less of a luxury for us, mere mortals. But for Air Deccan, air travel would have continued to be out of bounds for the bulk of India's population.

I met Capt. Gopinath in the chic lounge of a five-star hotel at a stone's throw away from Mumbai's international airport, one late evening last year. It was one of those sweltering evenings in the city and while I, anxious that I would be late, arrived before time, he was caught in traffic in south Mumbai. In the forty-five minutes that I waited, I realized what it is that has made him a much-respected and admired figure in India and, indeed, elsewhere in the world.

Capt. Gopinath is a man of remarkable humility, a man who does not hesitate to say sorry if he has goofed up or inconvenienced anyone. There are few men of his stature and achievements who would even think of apologizing for keeping somebody waiting. He kept up a steady update via text messages, telling me about his whereabouts and expected time of arrival. It is not difficult to imagine where the airline that he started, got its work and service ethic from!

Despite the fact that he set up an airline business whose market capital touched US$1.1 billion in just four years of its launch, Capt. Gopinath is a remarkably grounded man, very much connected to the way the masses in India live. As I listened aptly, fascinated by the story of the humble village school teacher's son from Karnataka who joined the army, reinvented himself as farmer, and then a serial entrepreneur, we gorged on a plateful of samosas and a sumptuous Indian spread of fiery, spirited Indian curries. Capt. is as feisty and spirited as the Indian curries that he has a fondness for.

Capt. is also a self-made man with a piercing intelligence, greatly interested in the lives of those who touch him. He is also startlingly well-read. To be in his company is to be exposed to the thoughts and quotes of some of the world's greatest minds. He reads voraciously, a habit whose seeds were sown in his childhood when his father home-schooled him and read to him about the lives of great leaders.

When I met him that evening, he was in the midst of hectic negotiations to restart Air Deccan, the airline that he had sold to another private airline. That deal had disappointed him because he felt the buyer had not done justice to his brand and kept up the spirit of the enterprise that he has started.

I asked him if it did not scare him to take on such a humungous responsibility when, in fact, he had burnt his hands a couple of time in business, wiping away a bulk of the wealth he had created.

This is what he had to say to me: 'For dreaming, he (Capt.'s father) read to me about Tagore and Gandhi, Nehru and Tilak, and he showed me the less fortunate people around me so that I always counted my blessings. He never gave me the opportunity to be envious of those more privileged. It was because of this that when I found myself living hand-to-mouth in a tent, I never felt poor. I had the arrogance of the wealth of nature around me. I never felt poor because I was so drunk with the possibilities of my life and never noticed what I did not have in my life.'

The village schoolmaster would have been proud of his son, if he had been around to see what he has made out of his life. Among other things, the Founder, Chairman, and Managing Director of Deccan 360, has been knighted with 'Chevalier de la Legion d'Honneur', the highest civilian award conferred by the French government.

To me, it is very fitting that a man who attributes his entire being to what his father taught him as a child, should write this charming, very candid letter to his two daughters.

Dear Krithika, Pallavi,

None of the stuff that I write in this letter will be new to you or surprise you because this is the stuff that I have always based my life on. You have grown up with me, have gone through the ups and downs of my life, and have seen that at every stage, I have done whatever it is on hand at that point with complete sincerity. We have had great wealth and enjoyed a life of plenty and we have also lived a spartan life in our farm when I decided to become a farmer and grow coconuts, areca nuts, and silkworms. And I know that every time I decided to do something new, your lives were disturbed by it, but you did it willingly and have enjoyed every step of the adventure and learnt along the way.

My dear daughters, as two young, talented women, I want you to know that the most important thing is for you to be intensely passionate about everything that you do. Don't be like a passenger on a train but be its driver. Be completely committed to pursuing your dreams but at the same time, let that not be an exercise in self-indulgence. Understand that everything that you have today is the product of your ancestors' labour. The comfortable life that you are able to lead has been made possible by their hard work and perseverance. So, while you are passionate about your own interests, let it be in consonance with the society. While it furthers your own fulfilment, it should also further the society's well-being.

I believe that passion and work are inseparable; they can't exist in isolation from each other. From knowing to doing is a journey in itself and if you lack the latter, any amount of talent is worth nothing. Make your life a journey of adventure. But if you are too much a person of society, you can't create since to be able to create, you need reflection and isolation. On the other hand, if you are completely isolated, you become a sponge on society, living off it instead of giving back to it. So you must know how to strive a perfect balance between the two.

Dear children, my father used to say that everything is rooted in action and that it is always better to lose yourself in action than in despair. The action in your life itself will then be the reward. The Scottish writer Robert Louis Stevenson once famously said: 'I travel not to go anywhere, but to go. I travel for travel's sake. The great affair is to move.' My children, every moment, everything that you do—small, big, significant—must be enjoyed. Happiness and wealth is a consequence of your actions, your ventures.

You should never be idle. Whatever you want to be in life, even if it were to become a cobbler, be the best one. Be obsessed with whatever it is that you want to do.

Nobody owes you a free lunch. Inculcate an entrepreneurial spirit and learn to stand on your own feet. In a marriage today, you are more likely to survive if you have your own passions, hobbies and interests. Mutually respect each other. Keep yourself both interested and interesting. Find salvation in your work. We all have to work for a living, but regardless of what else you do, engage in physical labour every day. When I left the army, I soiled my hands every day in my farm, did hard physical work, milked cows, and mixed manure. Though over a period of time I took a divorce from that lifestyle, I know that the bricklayer, the welder, the mason, the waiter—these are the true sons of the soil.

It is important to find good, meaningful work because it is integral to our happiness. Regardless of love, family, friendship, and other things in life, you will never be happy *if you don't have work. Make sure that the work must be one that enlarges the well-being of the community around you. Remember that your love for work should not be in conflict with the love for the community in which you have been raised.*

When you both were in college, I gave you the freedom to choose the subjects of your choice. I'm sure you remember what I had told you then: 'While you are free to discover your passions, I won't appreciate idleness of the mind and body.'

Dear Pallavi, you went to the UK to do your masters in literature and while you were there, you were true to your word, working as a waitress in a restaurant to supplement the limited money I gave you. And you continued to do so for three years before leaving for Birmingham for a Masters in Media degree. Do you remember the day we were dining with the Chief Commercial Officer of Airbus, John Leahy and he offered you a one year global internship? You were confused and taken aback because your thesis was yet to be finished. I vividly remember telling you how it's not important to have a degree but get the maximum experiences you can in your lifetime. And so you went and lived in France for a year, learning about another culture, another way of life. That internship enchanted you enough to make you want to do an MBA in Aerospace management. When I asked you to come back to India at that point, it was because I was starting my company, Deccan Air Cargo and Express Logistics, and I knew it would be a great way for you to learn about doing business in India—you saw the challenges, the joys and the frustrations of trying to float a start-up enterprise in this country.

Despite having studied abroad and having been exposed to the best education models, I am convinced that life has been the biggest teacher for you. You were both born on our farm at a time when your mother and I were extremely young and just learning to handle the responsibility of two girls. You would accompany me on my bullock cart to the farm and into the village, learning to enjoy the greenery and fresh air, prancing around without shoes, and attending the village school. At one point we even lived in a tent, out in the open. Later, when you were both still around 10 years of age, we shifted to Bangalore and you lived the urban experience.

My life itself has been my biggest adventure and you have had a ring-side view of it. After I resigned from the army, unable to cope with the ravages of war and its effect on my mind, I motorcycled through the length and breadth of the country and hitchhiked in the US. At 27, there was a kind of restlessness within me that I was unable to quell. I had led a full life, lived in the Himalayas for two years, experienced a war, and was longing to go back to my village. When I got there, I found the government had built a dam across the river and so my father's small plot of land had been submerged by the waters. The compensatory land they had given my father was remote, about a hundred kilometres away. It had no water, no power, nor an approach road. But I did not find any of this intimidating. For me it was more romantic than anything else. I wanted to work with my hands on the soil, be alone, take long walks, read, raise cows, and grow crops. I was like a man possessed. Bitten by the farming bug, I went to Bangalore, bought a tent, a Doberman dog, enlisted the support of a village harijan boy to herd cattle, and went to the barren land to pitch my tent on my piece of land in the middle of nowhere. For two years I lived and breathed only that.

That has been the mantra of my life, dreaming and deciding the course that my life would take. That is how I joined the army, and subsequently Air Deccan airlines was born, and that is how I went back to farming. That is also how I founded the air cargo business a few years ago and I am now on course to restart Air Deccan.

Dear daughters, there is no recipe for success in life. Every day I get letters in the mail from people who want to know how I became successful. I just tell them to live their dream, whatever it may be, with passion and hunger. Have an inextinguishable optimism about yourself and things will fall in place. I never believed in failure and so I kept acquiring more businesses without fearing risk. In each of my ventures, that optimism propelled me and when things went wrong, I continued nevertheless, knowing I would survive. Things would ultimately reach back to near-normal. Hope always kept me afloat and alive and I always found a straw that I could grasp to survive.

It is the law of nature that at the height of our success the seed of decline is sown because suddenly you don't want to take risks and lose what you have painstakingly built up. I believe each of us has to go through the cycle of success and failure. Your will is what will take you through life's vagaries.

My father never sent me to school in childhood. The first time I went to school was in the fifth standard and I was never the worse for it because he taught me at home. Instead, he would take me to the fields and would show me the harijan way of labour. My father himself was a poor school teacher but he was better off than the harijans. He brought up seven to eight village children in the house who he would feed out of his small salary of Rs 90 per month. He never told me to emulate or aspire to be the village sahukar or the rich baniya, but he would show me the strength of character of the hard working peasant in the farm. He would point to the labour working in the slush in the fields and he would say: 'They have nature's bounty, free food, the blessing of being in the midst of nature'. He would read to me about the lives of Tagore and Gandhi, Nehru and Tilak, and he showed me the less fortunate people around me so that I always counted my blessings. He never gave me the opportunity to be envious of those more privileged. It was because of this that when I found myself living hand-to-mouth in a tent, I never felt poor. I had the arrogance of the wealth of nature around me. I never felt poor because I was drunk with the possibilities of my life and never noticed what I did not have.

As you set forth in life, I want to tell you that self-assurance and self-reliance are the most important things, especially for a woman. Believe in yourself and in the ability to stand up for what you feel is right. Don't be apologetic for standing up for the values you believe in. Don't follow the herd mentality; instead, visualize clearly what you want and ever so often, the light will shine through to you and make it clear to you what is the right thing you should be doing. Don't conform to the norm just because everybody is doing or saying the same thing. A firm resolve to follow your heart's unshakeable belief is an essential tool for a good life. You have only look at Sita, Rani Laxmibai, Chennama, Florence Nightingale—all those who had an overreaching allegiance to their own belief that ultimately led them on their paths.

You should be creative in life. By this I don't mean you have to go out of your way and do the impossible. Only once in a lifetime can one do some path-breaking things like the creation of the telephone or the light bulb. By creativity, I mean doing things by applying your mind to the way you lead your everyday life. Be passionate about things other than your work. Learn and enjoy music, books, environmental protection, contribute to preserving and enjoying nature. Go on a trek, stand and stare, go river rafting, cultivate things that give you joy in your everyday life.

Be spiritual not in the ritualistic manner but in the way you lead your life—celebrate and have wonderment about the way things have come together on such a grand scale in this world. Reflect every day and discover the meaning of life on your own. That is a journey in itself.

I am often asked if I believe in destiny. I am not sure about destiny and what is ordained for you. Our lives pan out depending on where we are born, how we are raised, and under what circumstances. If I had been born in Pak-occupied Kashmir and raised there, my life would probably be different and so would it be if I was born in a poor family in a backward caste in India. The debate between nature and nurture will continue but what I know is that sometimes the cards that you have dealt with is ordained but how you deal them is in your hands. I agree that destiny has a huge role to play in our lives, but what you make out of your circumstances is a lot in your control.

I was born in a family of less than modest means but have a lot today at my disposal, much more than I or my parents could ever have imagined for me. And while I don't want to lecture you about anything, don't be guilty about spending the wealth you have because I believe if everyone was to be simple, there will be no economic activity. Personally, I try to be as simple as possible. Simplicity makes happiness more possible than complexity, I think.

I still farm whenever I get time. At one time I was the largest silkworm producer in the country, grew coconuts and areca nuts. I miss that life and I plan to go back to it in sometime.

In the end, I want to tell you that a successful life is achieved being happy doing whatever you want in a way that enhances the happiness of others and yourself. If all hurdles have to be overcome, we will never get ahead in life. We have to just go ahead, take the plunge, and trust that the future will take care of itself.

Now, go ahead and live your dreams to the fullest.

Yours with love,
Papa

Chanda Kochhar

Nothing in the initial years of Chanda Kochhar's life, growing up as one among a college professor's three children in the desert city of Jaipur, ever suggested she would one day make it to *Forbes* '100 Most Powerful Women in the World' list four times in a row.

Destiny kicked in when her 51-year-old father passed away unexpectedly, leaving all three children in the sole care of their mother who had, till then, led a sheltered existence. The resilient homemaker called on her inner strength and took a giant leap of faith, moving the family to Mumbai where she picked up a job and put her kids through college.

'It was a very different life from the one we lived in Jaipur but she (mother) took up a job designing for a garment company, pulling on her inner strengths and making sure that step-by-step she put all 3 of us through college, got us married and set us up on our way.'

Chanda obtained a Masters' degree in Management Studies before joining ICICI as a management trainee, steadily working her way up the corporate ladder. At 47, she became its first woman MD and CEO, and its youngest too. Today, she is the captain in charge of $100 billion of the bank's assets and over 2,700 branches spread across 19 countries.

And yet, Chanda believes that each of us can write our

own destiny, largely by following a value system based on the tenets of hard work and commitment. 'Your destiny is what you make of it', the slightly-built woman told me at her plush office at ICICI's corporate headquarters in Mumbai last year.

It is hard to discount what she says because her career graph speaks volumes about the fact that she practices what she preaches. It was relentless hard work, along with the ability to continuously push her own boundaries, which ultimately worked to her advantage, and got her the top job at the bank in a keenly contested race between three highly talented women in the group. Chanda herself attributes her success to the fact that she is able to withstand extreme levels of pressure without caving in or displaying that stress to others.

But her journey to the top was no smooth ride and came with its own set of challenges. When the global financial meltdown led to a Rs1,050-crore decline in the bank's profit after tax for FY 2008/09, it was Chanda, then Managing Director, who stepped in to take some hard decisions. 'In times of crisis, the leader should broaden his shoulders and straighten his back so that he can absorb all the strain and leave the team to do their best to resolve the crisis,' so is her leadership mantra. It worked wonders for the bank and got her the ultimate reward: the privilege of stepping in as CEO and MD.

Chanda's biggest life lessons were learnt from her parents. Her father refused to bend the rules even for his own son seeking admission into the engineering college of which he was the Principal. And her mother single-handedly charted the course of her family's life without once letting her children gauge the extent of the pressure she shouldered.

It was from her that she learnt the importance of never letting stress get to you and, in turn, affect those who depend on you for leadership and guidance—whether at home or at work.

Chanda writes a touching letter to her daughter Aarti about the importance of family in our lives and of never letting the daily pressures of life bog us down.

Aarti is an engineering graduate from the University of Pennsylvania, Philadelphia and is currently employed with Boston Consulting Group (BCG) as an Associate. She plans to do an MBA sometime later this year.

Dear Aarti,

It makes me feel so proud today to see you standing in front of me as a confident young woman right on the threshold of an exciting journey through life. I am looking forward to seeing you grow and flourish in the years ahead.

This moment has also brought back memories of my own journey, and the life lessons I learnt along the way. When I think of those times, I realize that most of these lessons were actually learnt in my childhood, mostly through examples set by my parents. The values that they instilled in my formative years gave me the foundation on which I try to live my life even today.

Our family of five, comprising of my parents and three siblings, lived in Jaipur, Rajasthan. Our parents treated all three of us—two sisters and a brother—equally. When it came to education, or our future plans, there was no discrimination between us based on our gender. Your grandparents always had the same message for the three of us—that it was important to focus on what gave us satisfaction and to work towards it with utmost dedication. That early initiation enabled us to develop into confident individuals capable of taking decisions independently. This also helped me when I started out on my journey of self-discovery.

Every quality that has stood me in good stead in life actually has its roots in my childhood. I remember an incident which as a young girl, had left me thinking of my father as a harsh man. But it was only much later in life that I realized that what I had mistaken for harshness was, in fact, his way of teaching us to lead an honourable life.

My father was the Principal of an engineering college in Jaipur to which my elder brother had applied for an admission. He had also applied to a college in Baroda to be on the safe side, but it was far away for us who had grown up in a protected environment all our lives. When the results were announced, my brother found out to his dismay that he had missed the admission into the Jaipur College by a mere half per cent but had cleared the Baroda entrance test with flying colours. The family was, of course, disappointed. At that time, my father's colleagues in the college approached him with the suggestion that the college start a system wherein children of the faculty members seeking entry into a given course be given a small privilege in terms of a lower cut-off level as compared to the others. My father flatly refused to implement the suggestion in the year when his son would benefit from the proposed new rule. It was a good suggestion, he felt, 'but the college could implement it from the next year'. I remember feeling very angry with my father and thinking how unfair it was on his part to deny his son something that was within his reach to give. But now when I look back, I think my stand on values, ethics, and governance today was, in fact, formed from that very incident! We got our initial moorings about fair play and honesty from him and these are the values that I adopted for myself in the long run.

I was only a young girl of 13 when my father passed away from a sudden heart attack, leaving us unprepared to take on life without him. We had been protected from life's challenges so far. But without warning, all that changed overnight and my mother, who had only been a homemaker till then, faced the responsibility of raising three children all on her own. It was then that we realized how strong she was and how determined to do her duty in the best possible manner. Slowly, she discovered a flair for designing and textiles, found herself a job with a small firm, and quickly made herself indispensable to them. It must have been challenging for her to shoulder the responsibility of bringing up her family single-handed, but she never let us feel like it was a task for her. She worked hard till she saw all of us through college and we became independent. I never knew that my mother had such a wealth of self-assurance and belief within her.

As a parent with a full-time job, one must not let work affect the way you relate to your family. Remember the time that you were studying in the US and the announcement of my becoming MD and CEO of ICICI was splashed across all newspapers? I remember the mail you wrote to me a couple of days later. 'You never made us realize that you had such a demanding, successful, and stressful career. At home, you were just our mother,' you wrote in your email. Live your life in the same way, my darling.

I also learnt from my mother that it is very important to have the ability to handle difficult situations and keep moving forward in life, no matter what. Even today I can remember the equanimity and calmness with which she handled the crisis on hand when my father passed away. You have to handle challenges and emerge stronger from them, rather than allow them to bog you down. I remember how, in late 2008, we were faced with a situation where ICICI Bank's survival was in jeopardy in the face of a global economic meltdown. The situation was being analysed with a hawk's eye by major media platforms and debated widely in the public space. The problem started at the peak of the financial crisis in the United States and resulted in investors and customers expressing doubts about the bank, given its exposure to global financial institutions. I got down to work, systematically communicating with all stakeholders—from the smallest depositor to the sophisticated investors, and from regulators to the government—that the bank was sound and its exposure to these institutions involved a small portion of *its assets. I understood their concern because so many of them feared that their hard earned savings in our bank could be at risk. Simultaneously, I also advised staff across the bank's various branches to lend a sympathetic ear to those depositors who turned up to withdraw their money, telling them to also offer the depositors a seat and a glass of water while they waited. And though depositors were welcome to withdraw their money if they wanted to, our staff also took care to explain to them that it would not help them to take their money away, because there was no real crisis situation.*

It was during this period that I took a couple of hours off one day to attend your brother's squash tournament. I did not know it then, but my very presence at the tournament went a long way in reinstalling customer confidence in the bank. A few mothers at the tournament came up to me and asked me if I was Chanda Kochhar from ICICI Bank and when I replied in the affirmative, they said that if I could still find time to attend a tournament in the midst of a crisis, it meant that the bank was in safe hands and they need not worry about their money!

It was also from my mother that I learnt the importance of adapting to circumstances and not being afraid of the unknown. In the 25 years that I have spent at the ICICI Group, I have moved across several responsibilities— from setting up new businesses around the globe to heading new functions within the company itself. When I was told to shift from corporate banking to retail operations, I personally felt like I was taking a huge risk because the bank's corporate business, which I headed till then, accounted for the bulk of the bank's balance sheet and profits. In comparison, retail was a very small business at that time, but I decided to take on the job and in six years' time, saw it grow from less than Rs 200 crore in 2000 to Rs 100,000 crore in 2006 in the bank's balance sheet. I learnt to always keep my mind open to new ideas and looked at each new assignment as an opportunity to learn and prove myself. Adaptability is a great asset to have because life is so unpredictable and things can change overnight for any of us.

I am often asked how I have been able to balance work and home simultaneously. I will admit that it has been a tough, sometimes exhausting, but extremely satisfying journey for me. Often, I would make it happen by giving up on sleep and on my 'me' time, tending to all the things that needed to be done so that my home functioned well even while I was at work.

While working hard for my career, I looked after my family, been there for my mother and in-laws when they needed me around. They reciprocated in kind with their unconditional love and support for my career. Remember that relationships are important and have to be nurtured and cherished. Also keep in mind that a relationship is a two-way street, so be ready to give to a relationship just as you would expect the other person to be giving to you.

My career would not have progressed the way it did were it not for the support of your father who never once complained about the time I spent away from home. Your father and I nurtured our relationship despite the fact that we were both busy with our own careers, and I am confident you will do the same with your partner, when the time comes. If you had complained and whined about my extended absence from home, I would never have had the heart to make a career for myself. I am blessed with a great and supportive family and I really hope you too will be as fortunate when you set out on your own!

I remember the day your Board exams were about to commence. I had taken a leave from work so that I could take you to the examination hall myself. When you realized I was coming, you told me how you were used to going for your exams alone for so many years. It hurt me to hear you say that, but I also think in some ways, having a working mother made you much more independent from a very young age itself. You not only became independent, but also stepped into the nurturer's role for your younger brother and never let him miss my presence. As you grew up, I learnt to have trust and faith in you and you have now grown into a wonderful, independent woman. I now use the same principle at work to make our growing population of younger talent take on larger responsibilities. I believe in fate, but I also believe that hard work and diligence plays a very important role in our lives. I would not leave everything to destiny. In fact, I believe that in a larger sense we all write our own destiny. Take your destiny in your hands, dream of what you want to achieve, and write it in your own way. As you go ahead in life, I want you to climb the path to success one step at a time. Aim for the sky but move slowly, enjoying every step along the way. It is all those little steps that make the journey complete. When I became the Managing Director and CEO of ICICI in 2009, it was a great milestone for me. But when I started my career and the length of my training period was reduced from twelve months to nine in 1984 owing to my good performance, it was a source of great satisfaction for me at that time! So, enjoy every step of your journey.

As you go forward, you will sometimes have to take difficult decisions, decisions that others might scorn. But you must have the courage to stand up for what you believe in. Over the last three years, I have made considerable changes at ICICI Bank to de-risk the balance sheet and position it for sustainable, profitable growth. In the initial period, this meant actually consolidating operations, slowing down growth, and re-looking at some business models that were not doing well. It was a difficult thing to do, but for me the ability to do it came from the confidence of knowing that I had done my homework, analyzed the issue, and figured out what was the right thing to do in the context of what was happening around us. Aarti, this is something I want you to remember—make sure you have the conviction to do what you know is right, and once you have that conviction, don't let sceptics distract you from your path.

I am often asked what gives me satisfaction. To me, 'satisfaction' means giving my best effort to everything I do, doing it not just to the best of my ability, but in the best way it could have been done. Excel in everything that you are doing, Aarti, and apply this to every part of your life—your home, relationships, and everything else that is either a duty, a desire, or an obligation.

Aarti, there is no limit to what a determined mind can

achieve, but in achieving your goal, don't compromise on the values of fair play and honesty. Don't cut corners or compromise to achieve your dreams. Remember to be sensitive to the feelings of the people around you and don't forget to be diligent about your work. And remember, if you don't allow stress to overtake you, it will never become an issue in your life.

As a young woman stepping out into the world, I wish for you to dream your own dreams, aspire for something big, and create your own goals. Remember that good times and bad times will be part of your life equally, and you have to learn to handle both with equanimity. Excel in everything that you do, make the most out of life's opportunities and learn from every opportunity and challenge that life brings along.

Lovingly yours,
Mumma

Deep Anand

By his own admission, Deep Anand, Chairman of the Rs 50 billion Anand Automotive Group, raised his only daughter, Anjali, to be the 'puttar' or son of the family. The little girl that came into the lives of the Anand couple after almost two decades of their marriage, brought renewed joy and meaning into their lives.

The couple, however, decided that their daughter would stand a better chance at being a global citizen if she went to residential school abroad. They saw it as an opportunity for her to make new friends, learn about new cultures, and share her blessings with others.

At the young age of 27, Deep Anand established his first business venture in the year 1961, setting up the group's flagship company, Gabriel India, which manufactured shock absorbers. Decades later, his daughter Anjali Anand Singh, mother of twins, is waiting in the wings to take over the empire.

Back from her wanderings around the world, which included a Masters in Fine Arts from Central St. Martins and a Business Management degree from the University of Westminster, Anjali Singh, however, remained restless and unfulfilled with her father's business and eventually set out on her own, setting up luxury resorts in India's rural outback. She is as proud of The Serai, a luxury tent resort in the Thar desert and Sher Bagh, an eco-resort situated in India's tiger belt of Ranthambore, as she is of her pair of twins.

Now in his late seventies, Deep Anand continues to be the energetic, restless young man that he was when he went about the task of establishing enduring global partnerships with leading automotive component companies from around the world. While the history of Indian companies and their global partnerships is replete with examples of failed relationships and bitter separations, the Anand Group today has 13 joint ventures and 7 technical licenses, all which have withstood the pressures of doing business in what has been a roller coaster ride in uncertain economic terrains. The group has since then become the subject of management studies on establishing long-term business partnerships.

In the fifty years that he has invested into the company, the group has grown to be a much admired entity, with 8 companies spread across 49 locations and 9 states in the country and a separate vertical operating in the Luxury Hospitality segment which was started by Anjali.

The key to his success has been his belief that it is people who make organizations what they are. Over the last few decades, he has honed and perfected the ability to take on board people from diverse backgrounds, with a diversity of beliefs and thoughts, to steer his conglomerate to success. 'Business is 90% people', he told me several times during our multiple meetings. The Anand Group employs over 13,000 people across its various locations and offices. The group lays great emphasis on the development of its employees through training programmes conducted by its in-house technical and management institute—Anand 'U'.

The young man who came from Lahore with a heart full of dreams studied Mechanical Engineering at the Chippenham College of Technology, UK, and started his career in 1954 as a Plant Manager with Mahindra & Mahindra in Mumbai.

When his father wanted him to go the regular route and be content with a small business of his own, he stood his ground and relentlessly chased his ambitions till he struck pay dirt. He continues to be the face of the group, travelling and striking up relationships around the globe, for the company's growth.

When he is not busy with work, Anand retires to his many homes around the country. I met him at his sprawling farmhouse by a river on the outskirts of Pune, with a few hundred mango trees, a swimming pool that he shares with wild ducks, and fruit and vegetable orchards that make the place a self-sufficient abode. During the course of our meeting, he showed me around the place in an all-terrain-vehicle with child-like delight while I hung on for dear life in the back seat.

Anand is also an avid reader and golf player who used to enjoy shooting game. He raised Anjali in their farmhouse in Delhi where she had the company of horses and spent her days collecting bird eggs and bonding with nature.

'I brought her up as my Puttar but today, I must confess that I feel the boundless joy of having a daughter. It is such a pleasure to have a daughter. She is more forgiving, caring,

and more than generous in reciprocating your affection,'
Anand told me about Anjali.

❧

Dear Anjali,

Over the last three decades that your mother and I have been
blessed with your presence in our lives, the one thing about
you that has continuously kept us captivated is your endless
diversity, your unlikely interests, and your boundless spirit.

We are not sure where you got it from. Your mother says
you got it from me because I myself was quite a wayward
child who refused to be reined in. But we are sure the years
of living on your own, from the age of ten when you went
off to Aiglon College—a British-based boarding school in
Switzerland—has a lot to do with the gifted young lady that
you have grown up to be.

It was difficult for us to send you away to boarding
because we were blessed with you after 19 years of marriage.
However, having studied in boarding schools ourselves, your
mom and I knew that the bonding that takes place with
other kids in that environment makes for lifelong friends.
The essential virtues of learning to give and take come easily
when you are in boarding, sharing a dormitory with other
children. Your mom and I were sure we did not want you
to lead a charmed existence at home. Aiglon College in that
sense was perfect. Your pride and spirit surfaced when your
Humpty-Dumpty figure made you the target of teasing; but

instead of buckling, you decided to dig your heels in and stay your ground. The teasing, in fact, seemed to have worked positively for you because you had proved to yourself that you were capable of much more, and went on to become Head girl of junior school at 14 and of senior school at 16. Before finally leaving Aiglon, you had made friends from some 40 countries, which in itself is quite remarkable.

Dear Anjali, that spirit has endured to this day. I still remember my amazement, and regret too, when I realized that instead of pursuing the Business Management degree that I thought you were going to take up in London, you had instead gone on to enroll yourself for a Masters in Arts at the prestigious St. Martins. Your heart was set on pursuing your passion for arts but you knew that I wanted you to study economics so that you could take interest in my business and take it to greater heights. But that did not dampen your spirits. You took your mother into confidence and for years you studied Arts during the day and pursued an evening course in Business Management at Westminster College, without me knowing what you were up to! And when I did find out, I had nothing but admiration for you.

Darling, when you came back to India at the age of 26, after 14 years of staying abroad, you were friendless and perhaps lonely here, but I am glad those times have passed and you have not just found yourself a splendid life partner in Jaisal but also given birth to a pair of infants, who you will raise, I am sure, with the same maturity with which you have handled yourself.

I know it has not been easy for you to integrate yourself

with my business but it has been very satisfying to see you apply your sense of intuition into it and learn from your colleagues and all the people who have helped me build the enterprise. You have proved that you are no dreamer with your head in the clouds but a down-to-earth woman with your head on your shoulders and feet on the ground.

Anjali, you have spent the last 4 years intermittently following your own passions—painting, writing, photography, and setting up home with your life partner. As you now take on the responsibility of raising your infant children, balancing the competing demands of marriage, two sets of in-laws, motherhood, and business will be another challenge. Especially since you will manage the business, the demands on your time and intellect will be many. I personally am of the view that a woman is much stronger than a man. When it comes to tough decisions, a woman is able to withstand pressure better than her male colleagues. It is not just raising the child, the process of birthing itself gives strength that most men do not possess. A woman is in several ways tougher.

I'm sure you have grown up hearing of my own childhood in Lahore/Shimla and our relocating to Independent India. My father and grandfather had a flourishing business in Lahore but when we reached Shimla, we had to give up most of our landed wealth. My father was a stern man, very hard to please, and he did not expect that I would do much good in life. My father wanted me to take up a job or any small venture and be content with it for life, but I had a bigger dream. In some ways, I think that was why I worked doubly hard all my life, especially in the beginning, building up the auto component business that has today grown into a billion dollar enterprise with operations across continents. Did I ever think I would achieve so much success that I would employee 15,000 people and have homes in several cities and hill stations of India? No. But I did have a dream in my heart and the desire to turn it into a reality.

I started with the automobile industry when it was in its infancy in India and that gave me a head start over the Americans, the Japanese, the Koreans, the French, and the Germans who arrived in India in this space. I remained miles ahead of them, leading a diversified group with over a dozen joint-venture partners across the world.

Darling, I believe discontentment drives us. That is what drove me to grow a small enterprise into one of the biggest names in the automotive industry and help it expand to different corners of the country. Complacence kills enterprise. When I'm content, I am most frustrated. You are just like that my child. Multitasking comes easily to you and I am warmed at the thought that you too, like me, will work ceaselessly for a dream.

And yet, you are different and you have a mind of your own. I was taken aback and a little concerned when, on your return to India, you balked at the idea of working with me and of living with your mom and me. You told me you tried and that you did not think it was motivating enough. You wanted to live on your own, follow your own dictates, and set up luxury resorts with your husband Jaisal, in the beautiful outback of our country. I may have faced some extent of despondency but I knew that over time, you would understand the value of what I created—Rs 5000 crore in revenue and 15,000 people working for the group did not come easily and I know you will appreciate it better.

'It will be different,' you tell me, Anjali, when I suggest that you do things my way. I have got used to that and come to respect your stand on shared responsibility.

However, I do know that the values you learnt while we raised you won't be different, because that is the essential part of a child's upbringing, the legacy that a parent can leave for his or her children.

My dear, remember the time you first told me that you wanted to expand your own venture and set up luxury resorts? I was a little despondent at first but I decided to set you free because I knew that in order for me to make you buy into any kind of business sense, it was important to allow you to follow a business that you loved. And I must say you did a splendid job, developing your first resort, a 100-acre luxury property, 'The Serai', in the heart of Rajasthan's desert land, toiling hard to get the project going, even with limited resources.

And when you found yourself running short of resources to grow and keep your business afloat, I was happy to have your business become part of the Anand Group, even though an auto component and engineering business has little in common with luxury resorts! I was glad when you saw the logic in agreeing to my suggestion since it gave you access to the manpower that we train within the group and also to the funds that our business can put into your project. Trained manpower is one of the biggest assets to any venture and

I am glad you saw the opportunity and seized it. In some ways, that has also brought you closer to the business that I want you to eventually oversee.

Two years back when your mother had to fly to London for surgery, you did a wonderful job standing in for me as Chairperson of the Supervisory Board of the group. You surprised everyone with how well you conducted yourself, took control of the meeting, and managed exceedingly well on your own. I was happy at your level of maturity and how you managed the egos of senior executives, most of who have been with the group for decades.

I don't know where this ability of yours came from but I am beginning to think it's got something to do with your involvement in art. It has made me re-look what I thought about your decision to pursue art as a career. Maybe the process of painting is definitive, there is a method to the madness. You tell me occasionally: 'Dad, you go all over the place when you talk. It is important to be precise and to the point.' I agree, now.

Anjali, the early years of your childhood was spent in the company of your grandmother, who brought you up gently but firmly, and you imbibed from her the Sikh way of life and grew up to be a caring woman who respects her elders and is concerned about their well-being.

It brings me to the point of one of my own biggest assets in running my enterprise. At 27, when I decided to branch out on my own, I was never left floundering.

Occasionally, you may feel you are not equipped for business, I want to tell you that at every step you will have good guidance. Besides, I am confident that you have great leadership skills of your own.

As for me, I think what has helped me is my ability to relate to people and reach out to them at every level of the organization. When you live alone in various cities of the world, as I often do when I travel, you realise you know nobody, you are a stranger. The millions in your bank do little for you. However, if you have created jobs for people, know their families, are concerned about their kids' education, that relationship itself is motivating and satisfying. I know you sensed and understood this well after you returned and you are quick to have adopted that interest in people. I believe our personalities develop with the challenges we face and that each individual is an embodiment of his accomplishments. My favourite theme in your growing years was 'Education is not everything. It is the only thing.' My child you have learnt well.

Sometimes, perhaps, you are too impatient with people. You don't suffer fools easily but I want to tell you that we have to do that occasionally. I would ask you to be less judgmental. We have an Indian way of doing things, in the sense that we take time over things, and you have to learn to work with it. People are most often inefficient but they are not ill-meaning and so, we just have to get them going and make sure they deliver. Business is ninety percent about people. Technology, marketing, and everything else make up the remaining ten percent.

Now that you are getting yourself involved fully in the family business, I know you will deliver. Nobody respects you for the money you have. Respect comes from building upon what your predecessors have set-up or something that you have built on your own and from taking care of the well-being of all the stakeholders.

Anjali, there are other important things little to do with business that I want to share with you at this particular juncture. All those years ago, when you lived in Switzerland, I, along with the help of your mother, decided to prepare you to live an independent life. You had a bank account of your own that you learnt to operate with responsibility and that came from the faith that we entrusted in each other. When you empower people at a young age, they learn to handle responsibility and authority. When you returned home after your studies, I confess I was concerned that you would not be able to manage money, largely because you were an artist; but when you started living on your own and handling your own kitchen, your staff, and establishment, you proved to be more than responsible and mature.

Put your faith in people, Anjali, and they will repay you with their commitment and loyalty.

I too grew up in a family of ten siblings comprising of six sisters and three brothers and as I grew up, my network of friends expanded. My closest friends even now are those from my school days. Some of them are now dying on me. I have lost a couple of close friends who I had known for over fifty years and if I don't make new friends, I am likely to be a lonely man. I have an American friend, Lee Perkins, who now follows the good weather across the country, living a full life in each of his five homes. I asked him once how he has so many friends in strange places and he said to me that it is a necessary art of survival. 'You learn how to make new associations and friendships. Not all will be deep and long lasting, but they will be good relationships nevertheless,' he told me. I think it makes good sense. At 86, Lee hunts, fishes, travels the world, and leads a more than active life, even at home.

As a woman growing up in a largely man's world, there are a couple of things I want to lay emphasis on. Don't let anybody take you for a meal without paying for it. Be financially independent, always. I know you practice this till today and I am proud of it, even if you sometimes do it with me too.

You grew up exposed to nature, spending your childhood gathering birds eggs on our estate and riding horses when you were a little girl of barely 6 and it saddens me that today you are no longer into sports, as much as you should be. I understand that arts and nature is what catches your imagination but I want you to understand that being engaged in sports is part of leading a full life. You know how a sport encourages team play and makes you tough emotionally and physically. Horse riding, for instance, teaches you alertness, develops your mind, and helps you to predict behavior—if you are not alert and watchful of the horse's behavior, you risk finding yourself thrown on the ground. I know in childhood you have had a few falls from riding on the horse's back.

Darling, I want you to live life to the fullest and cultivate a variety of interests. Being multi-faceted is a very important part of being a successful human being. Today, when several of my friends are retired from active professional lives and sitting in their clubs playing cards, I find myself unable to do that. Perhaps, if I had learnt the art of killing time at a young age, I would have enjoyed it but my youth was spent in building up my career with the result that today, I don't even know how many cards a pack has! I know it has two Jokers! Thankfully, I have my own pet passions—Golf, movies, music, reading, watching an occasional play—which adds so much value to life. Let us not overlook my addiction to Italian, Chinese, Japanese, and Indian cuisine.

My letter to you will remain incomplete if I don't tell you what you mean to your parents. The five years that you spent with us after you returned home from your studies was such a precious period, one in which I felt like you were ours, finally. That was also when we talked business, you and I. I know you are a private person and shared more about the man you were seeing then with your mom than with me, but just getting to talk with you about life in general and business matters was hugely interesting for me.

Happiness, I've always felt, comes from following your heart. Today I think that going into a different line will maybe will open up vistas for me that I would never have seen, but for your prodding. I am looking forward to spending time with you, so you will be able to teach me things that I never learnt from anywhere else. With a child, especially with a gifted daughter like you, learning can be fun. I've already learnt so much just by watching you conduct yourself.

I have learnt to love from you. Having you and loving you

brought another dimension to my definition of love, taught me of a love that is pure, taught me to be more considerate, more appreciative and understanding. Adults can learn from a child's love; there is no give and take there, just joy and complete acceptance. From you, I learnt what it is to love unconditionally.

Dear Anjali, I brought you up as the son of the family, 'my puttar'. But now, it is such a pleasure to have a daughter. She is more forgiving, caring, and more than generous in reciprocating your affection.

Maybe I never told you this before but sometimes I dream of you sitting next to me, listening to my rambling nonsense, and not disappearing to cater to all the other distractions in your life. I love your attention, dear daughter. I want to enjoy your company. There are too many distractions that take you away from me and your mother, like the phone constantly buzzing by your side. I want to ask you, do you know where the birds sat before mobiles phones were invented? On telephone wires that no longer exist. Now you know why I don't possess a mobile. But you have not noticed and I have not asked you, because there are always too many distractions for us to have the time to share that.

With all my love,
Dad

Ganesh Natarajan

Ganesh Natarajan's earliest lessons were learnt from his father, a simple village boy who worked relentlessly to make a career for himself so that he could look after his parents and thirteen siblings . That journey took the young man from his village in the state of Tamil Nadu to the city of Kolkata where he set up a small enterprise, and from there to, Tatisilwai, a small village in what is now the state of Jharkhand.

His father's commitment to his family and to the people around him left a lasting impression on Ganesh. As a young man, he recalls evenings spent serving up milk to the children of the village and joining them in singing patriotic songs which, his father told him, would make them better human beings. From his father, who worked hard at the factory and then at the Ramakrishna Mission's Seva Kendra till late night, Ganesh learnt the qualities of sincerity, hard work, love for the community, and the ability to maximize his time. From his mother and grandmother, he learnt generosity of heart and the ability to make the whole world his own and to reach out to everyone who touched his life.

Today, Ganesh Natarajan is the Vice-Chairman and CEO of Zensar Technologies, one of the most successful IT companies in the country, Co-Chairman of the National

Knowledge Council, and a member of the Chairman's Council, NASSCOM.

The little boy who grew up to be a God-fearing young man now finds himself an atheist, increasingly questioning his earlier beliefs, thanks to daughter Karuna, a keen science scholar who is currently engaged in cutting edge research in Hematology and Oncology at the prestigious Harvard University.

Ganesh writes a nostalgic letter to Karuna, a letter in which he wonders if he could have, perhaps, spent a little more time with her during the few years that she was with them, before setting out in her early teens, on a trans global journey that took her to some of the biggest educational institutes in the world, including the Cambridge University. And yet, he says in his letter, he is glad they had the courage to let her find her own wings and take off in pursuit of her dreams.

My dear Karuna,

As always, it is a pleasure to write to you, this time especially so since you have now embarked on the next phase on your voyage of scientific discovery. In your fellowship at Harvard where you are working on Hematology and Oncology, I am sure you will put both your medical training and research orientation, acquired at the Cambridge Medical & PhD programme, to good use.

Your mother and I have watched you with pride over the last decade and more, from the time you were just another schoolgirl at Maneckji Cooper School in Mumbai to the education odyssey that has taken you through the International Baccalaureate programme at the United World College, USA, the Medical and PhD programs at Cambridge University, and now to the super specialization and post-doctoral training at Harvard.

Your travels around the world and your life experiences have made you a mature, wise woman, leaving me with little scope for sermons. Still, I would love to leave you with a few of my thoughts, which I am hoping you will assimilate into your own worldview. Over the years, you have developed a healthy respect for our own academic and business accomplishments, a better understanding of our roots, and of our journey to the current state of relative success, and I am sure this will inspire some of your future thoughts and actions.

My own family came from a little village called Vadiveeswaram in the Nagercoil district of Tamil Nadu. My paternal grandfather, Ganapathy Iyer, was the headmaster at the local village school. But even though he was a working man, he never had enough money to feed and clothe his fourteen children. It was left to his eldest son Natarajan, my father, to take up the responsibility of pulling out the family from their abject rural poverty to a life of dignity in the city.

You knew your grandfather very briefly and I probably never told you about the tribulations and aspirations of the young man who did so much, not just for his family but also *for industry and society. Having managed to get himself a BSc (Physics) degree from St Joseph's College in Trichy, he moved his large family to Kolkata when India was in the midst of getting her independence from an oppressive regime. Always a curious scientist—I suspect you get your interest in science and research from him—he co-founded Waxpol Industries in collaboration with the Garg family and went on to get many industrial chemical discoveries to his credit. Even today, people remember the famous Waxpol Car Polish and the industrial greases and lubricants that he created. Such was his simplicity and passion for work that he called himself Chief Chemist instead of Director (Technical) of the company.*

His humility was something he passed on to all of us. His friends were ordinary people that he worked with and so it was with us. Having discharged the eldest son's responsibilities by taking care of his parents till their demise, ensuring good marriages for his seven sisters, and jobs for the three brothers, Appa moved his little family of four to Ranchi to set up the Waxpol factory there and thus found the time to indulge in his many talents.

In Ranchi, our school-going days were spent in the company of the simple folks of Tatisilwai where we lived in the only brick house that the village could boast of. But our relative prosperity did not stop us from mingling happily with the village kids, indulging in hearty games of gilli danda. Appa was a passionate follower of the Ramakrishna Mission and he made sure that his entire family participated wholeheartedly in the Seva Kendra that he set up outside our family compound. Each evening, it became our duty to gather the village kids and feed them milk after which we would all join them in singing patriotic songs so that we would all become better human beings!

He had an incredible amount of energy and slept very little. He held the belief that life was so full of things that he had just time for four hours of sleep. He was my inspiration and he always told me: 'Life is a gift and I don't want to idle away time. It is a waste of my intellect and education.'

He was also the life and soul of the Tamil Sangam, (an informal cultural body of the local Tamil population) and brought some of the best artistes, philanthropists, and seers of those times, including MS Subbalakshmi, Kamala Lakshman, Ghanshyam Das Birla, and Jayendra Saraswati, the Shankaracharya of Kanchi, to the little Bihar town and to our humble home.

When I think about it, I am convinced that his enthusiasm for life, his interest in people, and his commitment to hard work rubbed off on me too.

Karuna, I used every moment of my spare time for something useful, such as reading and educating myself. You are in Harvard today with some of the most intelligent minds from around the world, for company. I'm sure you are using that opportunity to increase the breadth of your knowledge.

Even as our little family moved towards relative prosperity and could afford a few luxuries like a monthly visit to the town's Kwality restaurant, the occasional Enid Blyton book, or the latest movie, we still stayed true to the values of leading a simple life that father advocated. I remember the time when the six of us from Seva Kendra were invited to sing the welcome song for Prime Minister Indira Gandhi's visit to Ranchi. The next morning, her cavalcade of over forty cars was to pass by our Seva Kendra and my father was convinced that she would stop and visit us. So we stood on the dusty road and watched the cars flash by when suddenly the PM's car reversed to halt beside us and Mrs Gandhi came out beaming and greeted all of us, much to our utter surprise! Your grandfather had complete faith in himself and in the greater power of doing good and this was one instance among many where he showed that such a power could indeed move mountains!

There is an old cliché that behind every successful man is a woman and nothing could epitomize this more than your grandmother Subbalakshmi, fondly called Rajam, who came from Bombay as a bride into our large family in the year 1951. She was a graduate who was encouraged by your great grandfather Ganapathy Iyer to complete her Bachelor's Degree in Education in Kolkata and became one of the most successful teachers of Mathematics and Sanskrit at the Bishop Westcott School in Namkum near Ranchi where both my sister and I completed our school education. She was the family's pillar of strength, a willing ally to my father in all his activities, and, later on, his source of strength when his health slowly failed him. She was also the guiding parent for both my sister and I, helping us through school work, teaching me cricket and music, and encouraging all forms of curricular and extracurricular pursuits. You did *have some experience of her wisdom and love during the years she stayed with us in Mumbai after your grandfather's demise, so you know how much she pushed for strong values and excellence. She was an inspiration to all whose lives were touched by hers!*

I learnt many lessons from the way my parents conducted their life and I think these lessons and values are applicable to future generations too.

My parents believed that you can never choose the hand that fate deals you but insisted that how you play the game determines whether you win or lose in the larger game of life. Shouldering responsibility cheerfully without regret or remorse is one of the abilities that separate true winners from the also-rans, they said. As a young man who had to look after the needs of ten siblings and his parents, he never complained about his fate or blamed destiny for it. He just worked hard and dispensed his duties with good cheer.

Appa always said: 'Don't let transient troubles come in the way of long-term goals. If there is something worth achieving in life, whether at work or beyond it, it is worth burning the midnight oil and pursuing relentlessly.' I second that completely, Karuna, and know that you are already living that life.

Never inflict your passions or priorities on others, my father said. If there is something that you like to do, something you feel adds great value to the world, others will gravitate to the cause voluntarily without any need for cajoling or coercion. This creates, long term converts rather than reluctant followers.

During your own growing up years in Mumbai, you would have seen many other examples of selfless endeavours that were worthy of emulating and you would no doubt have your own role models at various stages of your childhood and youth. Your mother's centenarian grandmother, who at that time was over seventy when you spend your first year with the family at Pondicherry, has always been a role model for all of us. The young widow courageously raised two generations of family, her own four children including your grandfather SV Iyer, and finally, her great grandchildren starting with you! That is an indication of the abundance of love and giving that reigns supreme in a large heart.

I wonder what it was when you were in your early teens in school that gave you the sense of purpose to start on your interesting academic journey. Was it your love of reading, through which you experienced many worlds vicariously, or your realization that it was scientific accomplishment and contribution to humanity that was more important to chase than monetary goals? Whatever be the trigger, the transformation of our child into a focused young woman intent on succeeding in her Bharatnatyam dancing, her literary accomplishments, and becoming the Head Girl of the school in addition to finishing among the top graduates in the all-India ICSE exams has been nothing short of extraordinary. I must confess, that it was with a feeling of trepidation that we let you choose your path and fly off alone when you were still shy of sixteen years to High School in the US. But we had then, as we have now, the confidence that your own intelligence, common sense, and strong sense of values and purpose would keep you secure and focused on the vision you had set for yourself.

Dear Karuna, values are themselves a transient phenomenon in a world where social mores, acceptable forms of behaviour, and the expectations of one's peers keep changing. Our family itself has moved from extreme orthodoxy and somewhat dogmatic beliefs to a fairly liberal view of the world and we have let you choose your own road and follow your heart and mind without fear of reprobation or disapproval. The width and depth of knowledge you have acquired, not just in your chosen scientific discipline but in a variety of areas, have enabled you to build strong convictions that have, in many cases, rubbed off on our own beliefs. I grew up as a spiritual, God-fearing man but your company and our various debates during cherished family vacations around the world, have finally made me an agnostic!

Karuna, both your mother and I have worked hard over the last few decades, setting up new companies and pursuing with a passion many new projects. This has also made me feel that maybe some of that time we spent was borrowed from time that we could actually have been with you. But then again, your mother and I think too that we showed you by example, what it is to follow your heart and take your dream to fruition. If our relentless involvement in our work—one that is very essential to our well-being—has played a role in forming the intelligent and independent young woman that you are today, I am happy. Seeing your own devotion to your calling and your work ethic makes us extremely proud today. Medicine is a calling that can change so many lives, Karuna, and we are proud you have made that call to change people's lives for the better on your own.

Karuna, if the measure of success is the ability to bring about a betterment in the lives of people, then you are already on the way to becoming a very successful person. Your mother and I have always tried to help people in our own individual ways because we are aware that life is a transient journey and the productive time at one's disposal to contribute to other people's lives is really short. We all have the opportunity to make a difference and yet, so few of us actually go on to do something for others without expecting something in return.

Achieving success in life is certainly not easy, Karuna, but then, nobody promised you a shortcut to success either. Part of being a successful person is also the ability to relate to people, build enduring relationships, and help other people achieve their goals. Your mother and I personally know and take an interest in the people who work for the organizations that we built in the last decades.

You yourself have spent more years away from your country and your family and have been the recipient of the kindness of countless people that you have come in touch with along the way, so you know how important it is for each of us to reach out to those around us and lend a helping hand. Be good to people, my dear. If the only way to success is by trampling on other people, there is no point in it. Competition will always be part of our lives but our success should not and need not be at the cost of other people's happiness. I am convinced that money, success, recognition are by-products of your life goals and life missions.

Karuna, your mother and I have worked hard to ingrain in you a sense of how important a family is in the larger picture of our lives and we are hoping that when you start your own family someday, you will remember to keep them at the centre of your priorities too.

So what are my hopes and dreams for you, dear Karuna, as you embark on the next stage in your career which will see you emerge as a mature member of an elite physician-scientist cadre? You should and will be successful in your own pursuits and I hope you will retain the love for humanity and the bonding with your colleagues that are always as important as individual career success. I am sure that in your own life partnerships and family matters, you will choose well and build a nest that will nurture and keep you happy in the midst of all the pressures that your global career will surely entail. But most importantly, I am sure that three generations of family who have been successful in their own right but still remained good human beings will give you the power to be a wonderful inhabitant of this planet in your own right.

I wish you all the best and the power to be the best you can be and realize all your dreams.

With all my love,
Appa

Jatin Das

Jatin Das is one of India's foremost contemporary artists. Born in pre-independence India in 1941 in the village of Mayurbhanj, Orissa, the acclaimed painter grew up in a joint family amid a large bunch of siblings. As a young boy, Das developed a keen eye and a passion for art and would spend hours in the fields and woods around his ancestral home, keeping himself immersed in drawing and painting. Often, he would wander around the village craft fairs, returning home with prized possessions—handcrafted, lacquered toys fashioned by impoverished artisans in the colours of the rainbow.

When he ultimately told his family about his intention of pursuing his passion for art, they were disappointed, partly because in those days, art was not an accepted profession to follow for sons from respectable families. A career as an artist was also seen as a low-paying job, not remunerative enough to support a family. Regardless of the opposition he faced, Das decided to leave home and study art at Mumbai's prestigious JJ School of Arts. Those were tough days and money was scarce, but the young man revelled in his passion and got other treasures along the way—artist friends from around the world and friendships that have endured to this day and have changed the way he looks at the world.

With an illustrious career spanning over half a century,

Jatin Das is revered for the honesty and boldness of his work. He is credited with 55 one-man exhibitions in different parts of the world. Das is also a keen teacher who has lectured at art and architectural colleges and museums like the National School of Drama and the Jamia Millia Islamia University, among others. A humanitarian sensitive to the human condition, he has often expressed his strong views on incidents of social injustice in the community on public platforms.

His fascination for traditional Indian handicrafts continues to this day. He is currently consumed with his grand passion, the JD Centre of Art at Bhubhaneshwar, Orissa, a private, non-commercial institution which celebrates tribal, traditional, and contemporary Indian art. The Centre will eventually house his large personal collection of handcrafted pottery, terracotta, old utensils, folk and tribal crafts, toys, tools, and jewels.

Over a quarter of a century ago, Das was presented with an antique, handcrafted fan (pankha) in Rajasthan. The beauty and the ingenuity of the pankha fascinated him enough to set him off on a quest to collect pankhas from all over the world. Das is today the proud owner of over six-thousand five-hundred fans and is on the way to setting up a dedicated fan museum in New Delhi. Along the way, his fan collections have been exhibited at the Fan Museum, London, the National Art Gallery, Kuala Lumpur, the Reitberg Museum, Zurich, and the National Museum, Manila.

In 2012, he was conferred with the prestigious Padma Bhushan award for his contribution to the field of art. But he believes that his journey as a student of art and life is a work in progress.

Getting hold of the elusive artist was in no way an easy task and took many months of first tracking him and then persuading him to write the letter.

At over seventy years of age, Das is a delightful man, fired with a passion about art and life in general, that people half his age would find hard to muster.

When I first mooted the idea of writing a letter to his daughter, he categorically refused, delivering a stinging lecture to me on the media and its intrusive ways. He castigated the folks who actively seek out the media and let their life hang out with all its warts and moles in public space, just so that they can get their names featured in newspapers.

The relationship between a parent and a child is a very private thing and not something he would want to share with the rest of the world, he explained. Not wanting to give up easily, I cajoled, trying to explain to him that this was an inspirational letter not just for his dear daughter, but for all the women in this country who could take life lessons from his experiences. I think that did the trick, along with the fact that I urged his actor daughter, Nandita, to contribute to the book as well. He would, I think, have smarted and bristled if the pressure had come from someone else but coming from his daughter, it was a request he simply couldn't say no to. When he did write the charming letter, he insisted that I call it a 'note to her' and not a letter, which is more of a personal exchange between a father and a daughter.

I am delighted to present the note that he wrote—full of

nostalgia, memories of his own childhood, of the years that he spent raising his children, and of his growing concern about the direction in which our world is headed.

In a world where balance sheets and bottom lines have taken control of our daily lives, this letter reminds us all that there is a world beyond the call of money, one where honesty, decency, and concern for the people around you still matters.

A NOTE FOR NANDITA

Preface:

One's family is a private space. The media today is intruding into the private lives of people, and the people at large are not shy or hesitant to spread themselves thin and expose themselves and their personal lives to the public. I, for one, strongly believe in the sanctity of the private space.

Children are very special to their parents and vice-versa, especially when they are little. And I reminisce those moments very dearly.

My dear Nitu,

I know you will be surprised to see a typed note by me, one being printed and read by others even though it is meant only for you.

Your childhood was spent in small flats, travelling between the urban cities of Bombay and Delhi. Contrastingly, my childhood was spent in the old, princely state of Mayurbhanj, in a large family consisting of five brothers and a sister. We grew up in a big house with a garden extended with ponds and a farmland where I spent my time until I was seventeen years of age. I remember my mother saying, 'No one has come today, I don't feel like eating'. Sudden visitors were always welcome with open arms.

When I moved to Bombay in the sixties, many of my friends came and stayed with me, though I was staying in a single room flat at the time. At twenty-six, I got married to your mother. You were born in Bombay. Eventually, we decided to move to Delhi and six years later, Siddhartha was born.

We lived in Nizamuddin, in a first floor flat with terra red flooring which I got polished and smoothened so that you were comfortable when you crawled. This 'house' became 'home' to all my artist friends who came and stayed with us. You knew all of them well and received their affection and caring.

My studio always occupied the largest room in the house. You grew up with the smell of turpentine and saw a painting grow day by day. I always painted bare figures and both you and Siddhartha were never shy about it. Poets and artists breezed in and out all day and friends from Bombay, Calcutta, and various parts of the world came to stay with us. Slowly, the Nizamuddin home in Delhi became a guest house.

I hope you remember all the happy times we spent in that flat. I was housebound because my studio was at home. I was not only the cook and the gardener, I was also the babysitter, changing nappies and feeding you all. Since your mother was working full time at the National Book Trust, I was fully in charge of the house. You may not know I changed your nappy many a times.

I remember my friend Paritosh Sen would always come and stay with us and would babysit you when we went to parties. At other times, we would bundle you up and take you with us to exhibitions and get-togethers. I taught you paper cutting and tooth brush painting on stencils. I vividly remember when we were at an exhibition showcasing artist J. Swaminathan's work at the Kanika Chemould Gallery and you told me, 'Look, look baba—Swami Uncle is also painting like me, the way I spray on stencils with a toothbrush.'

Many of my artist friends' children and you grew up together. Ramachandran and Chameli's daughter, Moli, and Paramjeet and Arpita's daughter, Boban, were your best friends. We had a lot of shared meals together and I still have several black and white photographs of that time.

For all festivals and vacations, we went home to Baripada, our hometown in Mayurbhanj, Orissa where you and Siddhartha (Nitu and Babul) spent quality time with my mother, brothers, cousins, and their children. At our home, all cousins were considered brothers; there was really no concept of a 'cousin' as such. When my mother was ill, you stayed back for a month to nurse her back to good health.

After my mother died, our visits to Baripada became less frequent. But the innumerable photographic mementoes were enough to remind us of the good old days. With both my parents gone, the family slowly disintegrated. Everybody moved to other parts of the country, and here in Delhi, we found a home away from home.

When you were tiny, I remember you trying to pull out a leaf from a plant. I had gently twisted your little finger and you had said, 'It hurts'. 'It must have hurt the plant too', I remember telling you. I never forced you to study or do anything. For me, you learnt and imbibed everything yourself. Whenever you got a chocolate, you first shared it with the maid and then ate it yourself.

You went to Sardar Patel Vidyalaya (SPV) instead of Delhi Public School (DPS) or Modern School. Your school had a very progressive curriculum that put a lot of emphasis on the importance of studying art and culture. Many of our friends' children studied there as well.

You did well in your studies and always had varied interests. You even studied Tamil and went to a village adopted by your school to do shramdaan. That is probably from where your notion of social work developed further.

I am sure you remember we had a Morris Minor, the round baby car which we had to push to get it started so it could take you to school. But since the battery would be weak, it would often die and I had no money to replace it. You would get angry as it had to always be pushed to start, in the process of which you would inadvertently get late for school. It was shell white in colour and as we drove past the neighbourhood, the children would always shout, 'Here goes the mendhak (frog)!' I have the Morris Minor all done up and bedecked now.

Do you remember for one of your birthdays, Leela (Leela Naidu, acclaimed Indian actress and wife of Dom Moraes), who had also designed your dress, bedecked you like a fairy to dance in her garden in Nizamuddin? Do you remember Dom was your godfather whom you would affectionately call Uncle Dome?

You learnt Odissi from Madhavi (Mudgal) for many years. It's a pity that you gave it up. I remember you joined the street plays of Safdar Hashmi's Jan Natya Manch. You took them very seriously. I went to see a few of those plays. They were very touching. I knew Safdar because I taught in the art department at Jamia Millia Islamia. He was a wonderful and gentle person, killed by political hooligans because his plays were strong, outspoken, and forthright. You were supposed to act in that same play when the goons attacked. But you were away at Rishi Valley, teaching. We were all shocked and stunned.

I never do paintings about events. But I did a large canvas in oil on Safdar, which was auctioned in Delhi at the Lalit Kala Akademi, and the money was jointly shared between SAHMAT (Safdar Hashmi Memorial Trust), Alkazi Foundation for the Arts, Habib Tanvir, and many others that had been set up in the memory of Safdar. It was the voice of the creative community.

You have always been actively involved in social work. I remember you travelling to the tribal pockets of Orissa and

Gujarat to work for the women and children there. You also learned pottery at Sardar Gurcharan Singh's famous Blue Pottery in Delhi. Later, you made a documentary on him called Imprint in Clay.

I never had anything special to give my children, kept no bank balance, no nothing. The only thing I did have to give them was my affection. But somewhere I'm sure you both share the ethics and concerns that I nurture. After your Master's degree, you took a year off and went to teach at the Rishi Valley School and travel across the country. You have worked on various films on social concerns, even with first-time directors, in different languages. But your first directorial debut Firaaq got me worried because of the socio-political undertones in the film which was based on the aftermath of the Gujarat riots. Though I respected your conviction and courage, at the same time I was scared for you because of the prevailing political situation.

On your first trip to London, you had lived with a very dear friend of ours—Maurine Ravenhall—and one day she had asked you to cook. Although you had never cooked at home, you had the taste of good food in your palate and you must have cooked a meal from this memory of yours. They raved about it.

This also reminds me of your first trip to New York when you had called me. I had told you, 'Beta, keep your head on your shoulders' and you had replied, 'Baba have you ever compromised? Neither will I.'

While I am writing this note, so much water has flown under the bridge. You have all gone your own ways. Now *you are a mother and you are going through what I went through with you. Nursing your child.*

I had never asked for favours all my life and I am glad my children have grown up with similar values.

I hope you are holding the hand of your little one in bed, as I did yours.

With lots of love,
Baba

Kishore Biyani

It is a difficult task to describe or slot Future Group
Chairperson, Kishore Biyani. Over the years he has been
described variously as a maverick, a rebel, a dreamer, a
risk taker, and the Rajah of Retail. To me, he is all these but
much more.

Biyani himself is an ardent student of human behaviour,
though I doubt he will ever agree to describe himself because,
despite the thousands of people that he employs for his retail
group and despite the fact that he hobnobs with the captains
of Indian industry, he remains a very shy person who prefers
mostly to keep to himself.

Biyani began his audacious journey to become one of
the country's most celebrated businessmen with a simple
decision to step away from his own Marwari family's
conservative way of conducting their family business and set
out on his own. The journey took him through the bustling,
crowded by-lanes of Mumbai's trading localities where he
went from shop to shop selling stonewash fabric to small
shopkeepers. Later, he manufactured his own fabric from
a ramshackle warehouse in suburban Mumbai and took to
selling readymade trousers. When retailers refused to stock
them alongside the imported brands that they sold in their
stores, he was so miffed that he set up his own retail shop.
Somewhere along the way, when modern retail and large

retail malls made their appearance in India, a large mall developer declined to give him space within its mall for the Pantaloon brand. That one snub led Kishore Biyani into the business of setting up a fund that would invest in developing malls for retail, not just for in-house brands but also all the big retail ones as well.

If there is possibly one thing that Biyani is most known for, it is for being the brains behind 'Sabse Sasta Din', the day when millions of middle-class Indians patiently wait for the doors to open at Big Bazaar, one of India's largest supermarket chains, to shop for all range of goods, including big-ticket purchases such as televisions and refrigerators, at rock bottom prices. Biyani gave most Indians another reason to celebrate January 26, the day of the sale. He allowed us to convert our junk into productive commodities by inviting consumers to exchange these with new products at his stores. Who does not like a freebie or a good deal?

Biyani's business empire is rooted in his belief in the Indian way of doing things and in his complete refusal to look towards anyone or anything for endorsement of his ideas. At the age of 10, he remembers visiting the annual animal fair at Nagaur, near his tiny village of Nimbi on the border of the Thar desert. The little boy saw that while the villagers struck smart deals trading oxen, cows, and horses, they also had lots of fun watching camel races, cock-fights, and puppet shows, eating street food, buying jewelry from local artisans, and dancing to the tune of folk music. Biyani's own retail brands today reflect his memory of that village fair he visited decades ago, which is why his retail outlets don't just sell commodities, they also give the consumers a place to socialize and have fun.

Biyani's success mantra in business as well as in life has been to question established norms, rewrite the rules, and redefine them. In doing so, his biggest role model has been Wal-Mart founder Sam Walton who set up the phenomenally successful retail model which is the average American's retail mecca. He also looked upon Dhirubhai Ambani, the founder of the Reliance group, as his original inspiration, a man who so fascinated him during his college days that he would often hang around outside Mumbai's Oberoi Hotel to catch a glimpse of the businessman who visited the health club at the hotel.

The boy whose horoscope predicted unusual amounts of good luck eventually proved that prediction correct, setting up an empire that sells everything from goods, groceries, consumer electronics, furniture, cosmetics, to books, insurance, and entertainment. Not to forget dreams.

Here, he writes a note to his two daughters, Ashni and Avni, with whom he shares a relationship that is more in the capacity of a friend than of a father with his children. Ashni is director of Future Ideas, the innovation and incubation cell of the group and uses her complex understanding of mythology, anthropology, and sociology to understand consumer behavior before the group rolls out new businesses. Younger sister Avni, an inveterate traveller, has backpacked through amazing, diverse corners of the world and picked up their culture and habits. After graduating in sociology from an American university, Avni

105

SUDHA MENON

is home now and is the brain behind Foodhall, the group's new gourmet chain.

Dear Ashni and Avni,

This is unlike anything I have ever done before in my life, including the years we have grown up together. But here are a few thoughts that I want to put on record, not for just the both of you, but for whoever thinks they can benefit from it.

Ashni, you are trained to be a thought designer. And from you I have learnt that the source of everything is in thought. Thought creates idea and belief. These in turn shape our behavior, life, and business. Both you and I have been firm believers in involving the study of humanities in business. We like to delve into anthropology, sociology, mythologies, and the cultural diversity of India and like to be inspired from these areas in developing the strategic thoughts in our business. Avni, you too are trained in liberal arts and in the study of social science, societies, and politics. I believe that your education and your interests give you a unique strength in developing new ideas and executing these in business.

Many times over the last few decades, I have been asked what is the key to my success, what has made me the person I am, and what are the secret business mantras I have adopted that helped me to establish our large business group.

To everyone I have just this to say. Everything I learnt about business, and about life itself, I learnt in the huge joint

106

family that I grew up in. I learnt everything about people and interpersonal dynamics from observing the elders in our house where parenting was a community responsibility and children learnt values from whichever elder happened to be around at various points in our lives.

I believe business education boxes people completely. I did not train the both of you in either accounts and balance sheets or profit and loss issues but I am glad I got you interested in humanities. While understanding the nuances of finance is very important, I knew you would learn these anyway while being involved in the business. If you had first learnt about finance or business in classrooms, I believe you wouldn't have gathered the ability to learn the softer aspects of life, the importance of understanding human beings, society, social trends and culture—all of which are just as important in a consumer business like ours.

At a superficial level, you may find that the world values the people who can talk suavely about numbers and discuss balance sheets. But it is my belief and experience that in the long run, it is people who matter. It is how you understand and interpret people, how you deal with them and inspire them, and how you lead and challenge them that decide how successful and happy you are. The training you receive in a classroom can only help you to an extent. Life has been my best teacher.

Ashni, Avni, you have both grown up hearing me talk about the importance of human values. I believe that the source of everything in life is our thoughts, vichaar, soch. For me, there isn't a separate set of values for business and *another set of values for one's personal life. All my values are intertwined and what I practice at home is the same as what happens between me and my team at work.*

To me, the study of human behavior is the most important. Once you understand how and why human beings behave the way they do, it is easy to learn business. But it is not as easy as it sounds because to understand human beings and their mysterious ways, you have to understand there is no absoluteness where human beings are concerned. Every truth is contextual. You have to understand that life is not black or white and that there are lots in between the two ends of the spectrum. If we look around us, we will see there is a constant worldwide search for absolute truth but in reality, I think no such thing exists. Each of us process information in our individual way depending upon our background and upbringing and our truth depends on our unique set of circumstances. If we are able to accept these simple facts, life becomes less of a challenge and more of a journey of learning.

I know I have been an unconventional father and ours has been an unusual parent-child relationship, where I have been more at your beck and call, being ordered around by the both of you rather than being the authoritative parent who has sought to impose rules in your life!

Ashni, I still remember you came to me once when you were still a teenager and surprised me to no ends when you questioned me, asking why I was so different from the other fathers that you knew and why I did not keep tabs on what you both did with your time, your pocket money, and your whereabouts when you were out with your friends! It has been a different childhood for you and I am glad it has been that way because the both of you have managed to carve out the map of your lives the way you want to live it.

What makes me happy is that our constant discussions on life, the Indian mindset, the lessons we can learn from our mythology, seem to have all come together to make you both very unique people with very clear ideas of your own.

Avni, I am filled with joy that you have grown up to be a person who is so widely-travelled and so welcoming of the amazingly diverse people that you have accepted as your friends from all over the world, during your studies abroad. Today, I am always so proud to notice the energy and sense of dynamism that you bring to your work. I am sure these will stick to you as you grow and reach new milestones in your life and work.

Ashni, you are a deep thinker and over the years, your in-depth research and what I must admit is a very unique study of Indian communities, their festivals, customs, rituals, and beliefs, has added immense value to our business. The customer insights that you have gathered and the way you have led the innovation and incubation team in the business gives me the confidence that you will always have a superior edge in any business that you pursue. In fact, sometimes the way you deal with situations and the way you ideate at work make me feel you understand life, our business better than I do.

But I also believe that this is the beginning of a long journey. I believe that as you grow, achieve more, and take on more responsibilities, you will have to be even more sensitive to the feelings of the people around you. My personal philosophy has been to never worry about what people think of me and also to never build expectations from anyone. In expecting something from someone, you are not only setting yourself up for disappointment but also burdening someone with the weight of your own need.

Though I have always encouraged both of you to think differently and celebrate your difference, I sometimes wonder if that has brought with it its own set of challenges. Even though you may think differently, you should always be open and welcoming to people who may not match up to your expectations. No one should isolate themselves from people, even if they may not match up to you intellectually. It is never a waste of time and energy to spend your time with other people. It may not be possible to be intellectually stimulated all the time but it is also not fair to expect everybody to be like you! There is always a balance in nature's scheme of things.

I grew up surrounded by academicians, designers, business people, and each one of them has left his or her individual mark on me, taught me something. My aim is to constantly seek diversity and I hope this is what you seek out too because then, life truly becomes your biggest teacher. Diversity is the fun in life. Trust me.

Dear Ashni and Avni, one of the most important lessons I learnt early on in life is the importance of opening up the mind to different thoughts, opinions, views, emotions; the very process of doing this is a signal that we are accepting of people and ideas that are not our own and when we are able to do that, the rest falls in place. The most important thing is to be flexible in our thoughts and actions and to have the ability to hear and respect other people's thoughts and opinions.

It is my flexible nature that makes it possible for us to have a no-holds-barred relationship. We never feel a generation gap between us because I learnt to be open to all kinds of opinions, no matter what age group that thought came from.

Is there a legacy that I want to leave you? Yes! But that legacy is not the business that we created. If anything, I want to leave you with the thought that life is a journey of learning and for each day that we are on this earth, there has to be hunger to learn something new, something more. As you set out on that journey with this belief, your approach to life will be different from mine. I wish and hope that you enjoy the journey of life. There is great fun in learning on your own.

With love and wishes,
Dad

K. V. Kamath

India's best-known banker, Kundapur Vaman Kamath, was a carefree young man in engineering college in a tiny coastal town in Mangalore when, one day, his mother taught him his most important lesson in money management.

The housewife who spent her entire life in the little town did not chastize her son when she saw him smoke cigarette in those days. Instead, she taught him a simple lesson about money that he adopted as his mantra for the rest of his life.

'Do you know the principal sum a person would have to have in his bank to generate the interest that you are blowing away in smoke? For every box of cigarettes that you buy, somebody has to actually work hard to invest that money to get the paltry return that you are blowing away in smoke rings,' she told her son who later went on to architect what is today the country's largest private sector bank, ICICI.

Today, Kundapur Vaman Kamath is the Chairman of Infosys Limited, India's third largest IT services company. He continues to be associated with ICICI Bank as it is Non-Executive Chairman. Kamath's life began in a small village in Mangalore where he grew up under the supervision of his grandmother, a self-sufficient woman with an independent streak, who gave him the first experience of just how much a determined woman can achieve. The mechanical engineer eventually brought about the transformation of a government-backed developmental finance institution into India's largest private lender but got his initial life lessons from his mother, a pioneering woman in the family who contested and won the local council election in Mangalore, when it was not at all common for women to have preoccupations outside their home and hearth. It is from watching her resoluteness that Kamath got his first glimpses of the true potential of women.

That young man is one of corporate India's leading lights, with an awe-inspiring reputation that precedes him wherever he goes. He is the man who has almost single-handedly mentored half a dozen of India's most admired women leaders, a group of trendsetting women who began their careers as executives in the erstwhile ICICI (In the 1990s, ICICI transformed its business from a development financial institution offering only project finance to a diversified financial services group offering a wide variety of products and services, both directly and through a number of subsidiaries and affiliates like ICICI Bank) who were handpicked and groomed to take on leadership positions as the developmental finance institution transformed itself into India's largest private sector bank.

In the years since then, it is a matter of great pride to him that one of his protégés, Chanda Kochhar, has taken over the mantle of steering the bank as its CEO and Managing Director while others have left to become heads of competing banks and financial service institutions. Much like a fond mother who might feel a temporary pang about her flock flying the coop, but takes pride in the fact that they have set out on their own individual journeys, Kamath watches with visible pride as his mentees take giant strides in the field of their choice.

The soft-spoken gentleman that I met in his office at the higher echelons of ICICI's corporate headquarters in Mumbai, carried his many achievements lightly and insisted that the journeys and achievements of the women that he groomed would never have happened if they had not had it in them to relentlessly push their own boundaries. Each of them had it in them to take on a challenge and get after it with a single-minded commitment that nobody and nothing could distract them from.

It is perhaps one of life's delicious ironies that his own daughter, a highly qualified young woman who left home in her teenage years to study and explore her own interests, chose to step off the beaten path and be at home to care for her family of three children and husband who is a very busy doctor. It takes a man with great conviction who will say that it does not affect him that his daughter's potential is possibly being untapped as she leads the life of a homemaker in an American town. It is to Kamath's credit that he supports his daughters categorically and without apology.

'Success means different things to different people and if you have decided that your career should wait till you have completed your family and given your children all the attention they need, then being able to do that itself is a measure of your success,' he writes in his letter to his daughter Ajnya.

~~

Dear Ajnya,

You might think this is a fond parent's indulgent letter to his daughter but to me, it is a conversation with myself about the things that I might or might not have expressed to you in all these years.

You know, of course, that when you were born, it was a very special occasion for not just your mother and me but also for your entire extended family because you were the first girl child to be born in two generations of our family on either side, your mother's and mine. And while we already loved your elder brother, your coming into our lives was an amazing experience—not just because we were all learning the ropes of rearing a girl child through trial and error, but also because you ended up teaching me a whole lot of stuff about life in general. You continue to do so, even more now that you are a mother of three children and seem to have a wisdom that comes from taking on that role.

Very often, I am asked this question about you: 'How does it feel to be the man responsible for grooming and mentoring some of India's most successful women leaders and then to have your own daughter opt to stay at home and raise kids?'

And my answer is always categorical. That I find it admirable you took such a decision with positivity which shows your confidence in yourself. Success means different things to different people and if you have decided that your career should wait till you have completed your family and given your children all the attention they need, then being able to do that itself is a measure of your success.

You live far away now, in the US, but on my every visit there, I see you bringing up your children in such a confident manner and am struck by your remarkable strength of character and your dogged commitment to all the things that are precious to you.

Seeing you with your children reminds me of my own childhood and I want to share with you the memories and lessons that I learnt from my parents. I hope these are useful for you as you raise your own kids, even if it is in an entirely different age.

I grew up in a much simpler world, in a village where my father was well-respected—not just because we had a family business manufacturing the famed Mangalore tiles, but because of his education. At a time when it was quite uncommon for people to be well-educated, he was one of the first people who went to England in the 1940s to do his post-graduation and ultimately returned home after a few years to take over the family business.

Like all teenagers, I was not very serious about my studies and often whiled away time with friends. He would tell me, education and not wealth, can take a human being to the next level and beyond his immediate circumstances. Also, he would say, one has to take leadership position early in life. He would insist that leadership is something that can be learnt, like everything else is.

I was not sold on my father's constant talk about leadership and throughout my high school days, I was happy to be cheering on others in my group who took charge of things. It was only in the final year of engineering that I suddenly decided I wanted to contest the election for the President of the Student Council. Getting elected by 2,500 students was an exercise in managing the expectations of that many people and the dynamics of various groups and it posed interesting challenges. It was when I managed to pull it off and actually got elected to the post that I started taking myself seriously and believing that I could actually become a leader.

My father's belief in the importance of leadership skills is also the reason why he put me in situations where I could learn. Every afternoon, in between classes, I would ride my motorcycle to the factory which was miles away and spend three hours there, learning the ropes before heading back to college. I was not very keen on it at that point but today when I look back, I see how valuable it was to have got that opportunity so early in life.

He often told me: 'Your true wealth is your education and that is the only thing I can leave you with. Education, and not money, will carry you anywhere in the world.'

After my engineering degree, when I told him that I would like to do my management studies at IIM, Ahmedabad, it is to his credit that he agreed immediately despite knowing that my decision probably meant that I would never go back to the village to take over his business. That was the degree to which he respected education. What I carry from him is the legacy of education, the push to be a leader.

Though I looked up to and respected my father, it was my mother that I was closer to and I learnt many valuable lessons from. As it stands today, I am often credited with *having mentored a handful of capable women at ICICI, into leaders who now steer various organizations. And while I insist that these ladies had it in them to become exactly what they wanted to be, my early brush with women and leadership came from my mother. She was an elected politician—a member of the district council—even before my father became one. It was only when my father decided to follow his business and also get more involved in politics (he went on to become Mayor of Mangalore) that she gave up her aspirations for and took a step back.*

She had clear views on women, and the importance of them taking on leadership roles, in whatever manner or roles that they played. In her own family, she was the thought leader, the person everyone looked up to when there was a decision to be made. I think she was inspired by her own mother, your great grandmother, who raised me till the age of four. I still have faint memories of my time with her. I remember that she had a strong personality and that she called the shots in the family.

I see that sometimes in you. When you decided to put your career in law and microfinance on hold so that you could raise your children while your husband focused on his career in medicine, it reminded me a bit of my mother's decision. But in your case, I'm sure we have not heard the last from you about the matter of your career. We know the efforts you have taken with your academics and we know one day all that will be put to good use.

There are other things that I picked up from my mother that you know are the foundations of the way we live our lives. One of the most important things she taught me is the value of saving for a rainy day and of living a simple life.

She was smart with money. During and after my engineering college, I would smoke cigarettes. She once asked me casually how much the cigarette cost and when I told her the price, she looked at me and said: 'Do you know the principal sum a person would have to have in his bank to generate the interest that you are blowing away in smoke? For every box of cigarettes that you buy, somebody has to actually work hard to invest that money to get the paltry return that you are blowing away in smoke rings.'

My mother and I had this conversation during the time when annual salaries were less than Rs 10,000. So what she was saying was that if she saved Rs 3000, she would get an interest of Rs 300 and she was asking me to think about how much of that interest money I was smoking away.

That was the only conversation my mother and I had on the topic of my smoking. It amounted to simply this: what I was earning and how much of that I was sending up in smoke. That simple 'ism' stayed with me and for a very long time it was the single yardstick on which I took every spending decision.

You will remember the simplicity with which your mom and I raised you and your brother. You got only what we could afford and the rest, we explained to you, was something you would have to do without. I am glad to see you raising your children with the same values, even though, sometimes, I think you are much too firm and stern with them!

Another unwritten rule in the family, but one that was

embedded deeply in all of us, was the importance of living honestly and without compromise on the values that we were brought up to believe in. My father's career in politics never reached greater heights because he was incorruptible, too starkly honest to fit into the system. He opted out of the system that did not allow him to be the person he was and the ground rule at home always was honesty and the freedom to be forthright with our beliefs. That has been a guiding light in my personal and professional growth.

Your mom and I saw a streak of this, the ability to speak your mind without fear, when you were a teenager of just about 13 and we moved to Manila where I had taken up work. Do you remember the time, a few years later, when I decided to move to Indonesia on another project? We were taken aback and a bit shocked when you refused to accompany us. You insisted that you would finish your International Baccalaureate (IB) program in Manila since it was your final year and you said you preferred to stay with family friends and finish your course.

Even at sixteen you showed us not just that you had a mind of your own but that you had leadership qualities as well—you had, on your own initiative, found out everything about the way your course would be taught in Indonesia and told us it would be detrimental to your academic progress, if we insisted on taking you along.

That was just the beginning of your journey. While your mom and I came back to India after a few years, you decided to follow your interests which took you to the UK for a brief summer school at Oxford, and then to the US to explore *your interests on your own. I think your fierce independence taught you a lot of life lessons that will not be forgotten and brought out your leadership skills too.*

Your mom and I remember the time while you were the deputy at the women's hostel at Smith College in the US and had to take a firm stand against the rampant partying and violation of rules that a few of the hostel inmates routinely indulged in. You were much worried about having to take a call on the issue. I remember the times you would call and discuss the issue with me but when you finally took action against the errant residents, it was entirely your own decision. It did not go well at all with everyone but you did not mind being temporarily unpopular. In the long run, you became a trusted and loved leader in the campus. Often, a leader has to take decisions that might not gain him popular votes but he has to do what he thinks is a good for the organization and for the larger community. I have learnt that it is possible to take charge of a situation and resolve it without aggravating hostilities. All you have to be is firm and stick to your decision.

This brings me back to the subject of your choosing to be a homemaker instead of following your career in law or microfinance that you followed for a short while. Often in the world, women who are homemakers are not given the same place in society that a working woman is given. Sometimes the work place is taken over by debates on gender inequality.

For me, the experience of heading an organization that has been home to some of the most dynamic working women in this country, was a journey of learning. Maybe growing up in a family with almost no women made me gender neutral in the way I looked at women in the work place. I think in the quest for seeming politically right, we have built a lot of biases into our workplaces, without realizing it. A lot of times this is because we perceive a situation different from the way the women see it.

A lot of times a woman, I suspect, is given a different set of responsibilities not because she cannot do it, but because of someone's belief that it is not right or fair for her to be asked to do it!

My first lesson in understanding that a woman looks at this differently came in 1996 at ICICI. I was the Chief Executive Officer at that point and it worried me when women employees would take late night flights back home or if they worked late into the night at office. At one of the meetings with the team, which included a sizeable number of women, I raised this concern and asked them about how secure they felt. All I got in return were blank stares; none of them even responded to my query. I realized then that it was best to alleviate our own anxieties about the perceived risk instead of limiting what the women colleagues were capable of doing.

Women have different approach to risk and their jobs and we (society or men in the organization) unnecessarily build stereotypes around them.

At ICICI, we did nothing special to get the equations right. We were gender neutral from the recruitment stage itself. But the honest truth is that not every man has the same mind and so the balance gets skewed occasionally.

Somewhere we let biases get in and the only way to avoid this is by being constantly alert and to not let that happen. The answer lies within us, not outside.

At ICICI, once the merit process was put in place, there was never any question of gender inequality. We had a merit and performance-based ranking of employees which was reviewed every year and people got responsibilities that they were capable of taking on. When this is done, you get to a situation where you are not conscious of a gender mix at the table at all and that is when you can say your organization has truly become gender neutral. It took us about three to four years to reach there, but it was well worth it. Despite the debate about the need for affirmative action at the work place, I am convinced that a 'no affirmative action' policy is the best way, but we have to make sure we too have a neutral mind while doing so.

Often, quick affirmative action is very risky and holds the danger of creating a hostile situation for the women colleagues at the work place. In the long run, I can say only merit works.

Ajnya, when I see you with your children, , I often recall my own childhood. Sometimes I may differ with you about your rather strict ways of parenting, but I also know that it is right for you to be firm with the children. It is only the grandfather in me that makes me question that.

Growing up, you have had your grandparents and your parents push you to take on leadership qualities and in many ways you did, displaying a fondness for experimenting with various things, such as learning Japanese, when it was not *fashionable to do so. Your mother has a strong mind of her own but she has chosen to take on a supportive role in our family. She raised you and your brother and maybe you take after her. She made it her full-time job raising our children and you are doing it now. I see how supportive you are with everything that your husband and children do. And I admire the way you facilitate everything by having a very clear demarcation of responsibility in running the house.*

Ajnya, you have learnt a lot of things about life from just watching your parents and your grandparents and I hope you realize that your children will learn their attitudes by watching their parents handle life. Children pick up from the parents their attitude towards the immediate family and their relationship to the larger community around them. How you treat the people around you will have enormous bearing on the minds of your own children and I know you will remember this at all times. The same applies for ethics and integrity too. Children look at their parents for pointers on this and what they see becomes embedded in their subconscious.

I would like to end with this thought that parents expose their children to several aspects of life and are unable to expose them to other aspects for various reasons. I think parents will do the greatest service to children if learning from seeing is encouraged. Lead your life as you would want your children to lead their life and watch them become maturer for it.

In the end, I want to say that I could have regretted that you did not follow a career path but I actually look at your decision to concentrate on your family with a tremendous sense of admiration. Nothing is more powerful or more worthy of pride than the sense of somebody's conviction and the courage to follow one's own heart. I'm proud of you.

Lovingly,
Dad

Mallika Sarabhai

space programme. Dr. Vikram Sarabhai from whom she got the gift of enduring positivity. At his insistence she did a business management degree from IIM, Ahmedabad so that she would help him set up great institutions that would exist without material considerations such as income and profit.

allika Sarabhai is a multifaceted woman, a restless, vibrant soul unwilling to be caged in by boundaries and societal restrictions. Her interests are many. She is dancer, choreographer, social activist, writer, publisher, and commentator. But more than anything else, she is a human being whose heart beats and feels for the women of our country, the unsung majority who live in rural India and silently suffer the indignities that an uncaring society heaps on them. Over the years, she has worked relentlessly opposing crimes against women through her dance-dramas, mobile dance troupes, traveling through rural India spreading the word against female foeticide, child marriage, and maternal mortality, among others.

Mallika herself grew up in a family of very strong women including her danseuse mother, Mrinalini Sarabhai, her aunt, freedom fighter Capt. Lakshmi Sehgal, and her great grandmother, a feisty woman who once single-handedly mollified and made friends with a rampaging mob working in the fields of the zamindaars, who attacked her home during the Moplah Rebellion in Kerala's Malabar region in 1921. The Nair widow waited for the mobs to arrive, cooked a meal for them, and sent them home, mollified.

The biggest influence on Mallika's life was and continues to be her father, eminent physicist and the father of India's space programme, Dr. Vikram Sarabhai from whom she got the gift of enduring positivity. At his insistence she did a business management degree from IIM, Ahmedabad so that she would help him set up great institutions that would exist without material considerations such as income and profit. He never lived to see his daughter give shape to his vision but over the last three years, Darpana, an organization that her mother founded, has been steered by Mallika who has made it a hub for catalyzing social change through art.

Mallika is remembered for her inspiring role as Draupadi, in Peter Brook's 'The Mahabharata' which ran for five years, first in French and then English, performed in France, North America, Australia, Japan, and Scotland. She has, since then, made several hard-hitting solo theatrical works, including *Shakti: The Power of Women*, all of which talk about the inherent strength of women.

This poem was written to her unborn baby some two decades ago. Anahita is now part of Darpana and a keen dancer herself, who accompanies her mother, and sometimes her grandmother too, on stage.

FOR ANAHITA

A lullaby

The mother hums while rocking a cradle. She stops, peers in and sings:

Don't sleep yet my little girl
For I have a story to tell.
A long one perhaps, a hard one too
But a good one that you will tell your bitiya.

There is a world around—
A world of fools and knaves
Of frightened men and mindless women.

They see us first as women
Not people, not humans, not normal;
Girls, women, bitches, whores,
Other's wealth, burdens.
Soon to be gotten rid of.

They'll say you're a curse
An unproductive mouth to feed.
They'll try to starve you, burn you,
Keep you out of school.
They'll try to keep you scared
And away from knowledge and power.

But they don't know the secret
That I shall tell to you.
The world had changed around them too
But they don't see it, so blind with fear

But you must know that you CAN
You can work, and fight, and talk

And dance, and learn, and sing.
All by yourself
Without their help
Without their permission
Or blessings, or guidance.

And then, if you wish, you can stretch out a hand
And take a partner who understands.

Don't listen to their limitations
You can fly, you can jump
You can run, you can write
Because you are a woman
In a world where we can stand alone.

They will fight, hurl stones and abuse
For you will be the light that breaks their power
They will starve you, try and throw you down,
But you will know of the light inside
That gives you truth, and strength and courage
And above all
A joy that they could never give
And never withhold

For I am telling you a secret, bitiya
That you shall pass on to all the bitiyas
The future is ours
Filled with joy
Take the light of the women of history

And the few brave women of today
To light the lamps
A million lamps
For tomorrow's women who are free.

Narayana Murthy

For most Indians, Narayana Murthy, co-founder of the information technology company Infosys Ltd, is a wise elder statesman, a man who is respected for his knowledge, and is revered by both his industry peers and his business associates.

And yet, Murthy has a delightfully gentle and vulnerable side to him too as he reveals in this humorous, touching, and astonishingly honest letter to his daughter Akshata, herself mother to two little children. Murthy wrote to me just a few days ago saying Akshata gave birth to her second child, daughter Anoushka, on October 25.

'It is quite a well-known fact that when a daughter gets married, a father has mixed feelings about it. He hates the fact there is somebody else in his daughter's life with whom she shares her affection—a smart, confident, younger man who gets the attention that was his alone. I, too, was a little sad and jealous when you told us you had found your life partner, but when I met Rishi and found him to be all that you had raved about—brilliant, handsome, and, most importantly, honest—I understood why you let your heart be stolen,' Murthy confesses in this charming epistle to his daughter.

Murthy's own heart was stolen the day he met his daughter, a few days after she was born at her maternal grandmother's house in Hubli, while he still a young man working in Mumbai. In fact, he says her arrival into his life changed him forever.

'Becoming a father to you, my dear child, transformed me in such a way that I could never go back to being the same person I used to be before. Your arrival in my life brought unimaginable joy and a larger responsibility on my shoulder. I was no more just a husband, a son, or a promising employee at one of India's fastest-growing companies. I was also a father who would grow to become a hero to his daughter; a man who, in her eyes, could do no wrong, and I had no choice but to measure up to those expectations every day of my life. Your birth raised the benchmark for every aspect of my life, including my work life. My interactions at the workplace had to be more thoughtful and measured, the quality of my transactions with the outside world had to be more considerate, dignified, and more mature, and I had to deal with every human being more sensitively and courteously. After all, some day you would grow up and understand the world around you and I didn't want for you to ever think I did anything even remotely wrong.'

I met Murthy in his new office in a tree-lined, charming residential community in Bangalore just days before his son Rohan was getting married to Lakshmi, the daughter of one of India's most respected industrialists—Venu Srinivasan. And yet, there was nothing in his demeanor that showed stress about the million things that he possibly had to get done, being the father of the groom. Instead, the small-built, bespectacled man who was the torch-bearer of India's rapid ascent to becoming an IT powerhouse, regaled me with his stories of bringing up his children—from fond anecdotes of tucking them into bed to telling them silly stories till they had tears running down their eyes—and plied me with endless cups of tea as he chuckled over memories of the past. Murthy might be mistaken for a rather stern, old-world college professor, but through the course of my interview, I learnt that he has a wicked sense of humor and an elephantine memory.

❧

Dear Akshata,

A regular April evening in Mumbai, in 1980, suddenly became special for me—I received the much-awaited news of your birth.

In those days we could not afford a telephone at home, and my then colleague, Arvind Kher, came all the way from our office in Nariman Point to our house in Bandra to tell me that your mother had delivered you, back in Hubli, her hometown.

'So, how does it feel to be a father?' asked Arvind.

I replied that, for the first time in my life, I felt the compelling need to become a better person.

For now there was someone in whose eyes I could do no wrong. Someone, for whom I'd always be a hero. Someone, whose life would be shaped by my actions. I told him I felt a sense of awesome responsibility. I suppose, Arvind could see that becoming a father had completely overwhelmed me.

Akshata, becoming a father transformed me in ways that I could never have thought possible. I could never go back to being the person I used to be before. Your arrival in my life brought unimaginable joy and a larger responsibility. I was no more just a husband, a son, or a promising employee of a fast-growing company. I was a father, who had to measure up to the expectations his daughter would have of him at every stage of her life.

Your birth raised the benchmark of my life, in every aspect.

My interactions at the workplace became more thoughtful and measured; the quality of my transactions with the outside world more considerate, dignified, and mature. I felt a need to deal with every human being more sensitively and courteously. After all, some day you would grow up and understand the world around you, and I didn't want you ever to think that I had done anything even remotely wrong.

My mind often goes back to the initial days after your birth. Your mother and I were young then and struggling to find our feet in our careers. Two months after your birth in Hubli, we brought you to Mumbai, but discovered, quickly enough, that it was a difficult task to nurture a child and manage careers side by side. So, we decided that you would spend the initial years of your life with your grandparents in Hubli. Naturally, it was a hard decision to make, one which took me quite a bit of time to come to terms with. Every weekend, I would take the plane to Belgaum and then hire a car to Hubli. It was very expensive, but I couldn't do without seeing you.

What never ceased to amaze me was how you created your own little happy world at Hubli, surrounded by your grandparents and a set of adoring aunts and relatives, oblivious of our absence from your life.

I still remember the joy I felt when I walked through the door of your grandparents' house on weekends to pick you up and hold you close. As soon as you saw me, you would switch your allegiance, and we would become one inseparable unit. Neither your grandparents nor tachi (her aunt Sunanda) were allowed into our inner circle as long as I was in there! Everyone used to be amazed by this and we would all have a good laugh. Of course, I would secretly swell with pride at your loyalty. Most of all, I felt so grateful to you for your belief in me that continues even today.

When you came back at the age of 5, we had a ritual of tucking you and your brother, Rohan, into bed every night. Mostly it was your mother who did it, but on the rare evenings that I came home early, I looked forward to doing it. Remember the stories that I shared with you on those nights? They were always about our train journey from Bangalore to Hubli and all the stations that came along the way. You were 5 then and Rohan only a year and half. Each time, I would add a new imagined anecdote that happened at a station, you two would be enthralled all over again. Do you remember the story about our trip to Krishnarajasagar, the jokes, that brought loud laughter even though they were oft-repeated? The three of us would be howling with laughter and your mother would stand at the bedroom door and look on, amazed at our revelry.

143

I am often asked about the qualities that I have imparted to my children. I tell them that it is your mother who shouldered this great responsibility and I am ever so grateful to her for bringing you up to be the fine individuals you are. She communicated values more by action than by talking about them. She taught Rohan and you the importance of simplicity and austerity. There was this one instance, in Bangalore, when you were selected for a school drama for which you were required to wear a special dress. It was in the mid-eighties, Infosys had just begun its operations, and we did not have any money to spend on non-basic goods. Your mother explained to you that we would not be able to buy the dress and that you would have to drop out of the performance. Much later, you told me that you had not been able to understand or appreciate that incident. We realize it must have been a bit drastic for a child to forgo an important event in school, but, we know you learnt something important from that—the importance of austerity.

Life has changed for us since then and there is enough money. But, you know, our lifestyle continues to be simple. I remember discussing with your mother the issue of sending you kids to school by car once we were a little comfortable with money, but your mother insisted that Rohan and you go to school with your classmates in the regular autorickshaw. You made great friends with the 'rickshaw uncle' and had fun with the other kids in the auto. The simplest things in life are often the happiest and they are for free.

You would often ask me why there was no television at our home when the rest of your friends discussed stuff they

144

watched on TV. Your mother decided early on that there would be no TV in our home so that there would be time for things like studying, reading, discussions, and meeting friends. She insisted that it was important to create an environment conducive to learning at home. Therefore, every night we dedicated the time between 8 pm and 10 pm to pursuits that brought the family together in a productive environment. While Rohan and you did your schoolwork, your mother and I read books on History, Literature, Physics, Mathematics, and Engineering, or did any office work.

It is quite a well-known fact that when a daughter gets married, a father has mixed feelings about it. He hates the fact that there is somebody else in his daughter's life with whom she shares her affections—a smart, confident, younger man who gets the attention that was earlier his alone. I, too, was a little sad and jealous when you told us you had found your life partner. But when I met Rishi and found him to be all that you had described him to be—brilliant, handsome, and, most importantly, honest—I understood why you let your heart be stolen. It was then that I reconciled to sharing your affections with him.

A few months ago, you made me a proud grandparent. If holding you in my arms for the first time gave me indescribable joy, seeing Krishnaa, your lovely daughter, for the first time at your home in Santa Monica, was a different experience altogether. I wondered, whether from now on, I would have to behave like a wise, grand old man! But, then I realized the bonus to growing older and becoming a *grandparent. I would have the joy of pampering a child silly! Besides, you know what they say about grandparents and grandchildren having a common enemy—the parent! I am convinced Krishnaa and I will eventually exchange notes and crib about you and be completely on the same page when it comes to criticizing you!*

Jokes apart, Akshata, having Krishnaa will bring home to you the magnitude of the job at hand. In some ways, you already know it. Remember that day when you wrote to me saying how, for the first time in your life, you knew that I was not completely crazy for calling you up almost every day when you were studying abroad, checking on your well-being, checking up on whether you were eating well and resting, and making sure you were comfortable in every possible way? I was amused when you told me you were doing the same with your infant daughter, checking on her every few minutes, worrying if she was fed well, and sleeping enough, even though you know that she sleeps most of the day and night! That is what being a parent means, my dear.

As you begin the next phase of your life Akshata, I would like you to look back at the time you and Rohan were growing up. Your mother, when she realized that her job as an engineer with a corporation kept her away from you both for long hours, quit the job and decided to become a college professor instead. She wanted to be at home when you both returned from school.

Do you remember coming home and regaling your mother with stories about your day at school, having a hot snack, and later in the evening going over your homework with her? I know career aspirations receive much attention in this competitive world. However, what was important in your mother's time will remain the same even today, despite the much-changed world in which you live.

Having a child is an eternal responsibility, Akshata, and having to simultaneously deliver a hundred percent at work is like walking a tightrope. You are lucky to be in a position where you can take a break from your career for a short period and focus on your baby. Hundreds and thousands of women around this country do not have this option. At Infosys, I have talked to young mothers who leave their little children at home and have to perform consistently well at the workplace. I am reminded of how you are balancing your act and that makes me understanding and considerate to them. The world admires a woman who brings a sense of balance to all the three responsibilities—being a loving wife, a caring mother and a competent career woman. I have no doubt at all that you will strike a healthy balance in these responsibilities like you have in everything else.

Tell Krishnaa lots of stories and instill good values in her through them. Tell her, like I told you, stories of the accomplishments, courage, compassion, sacrifice and adventure, of your aunts, uncles and grandparents. Through them she will know her ancestors intimately and be inspired by their lives. It is also how she will develop love and respect for your elders and make a bond with the past and the present.

As you pursue your goals and live a contended life,

remember that there is only one planet for us to live in and that planet is now becoming endangered. Remember that it is your responsibility to pass on this planet to Krishnaa in a better condition than you got it from us.

The world is yours to explore. Right from the beginning, your mother and I felt that it would be so much better for you to create your own future. You are already the entrepreneur you wanted to be. You will be putting India's crafts and textiles tradition on the global map with your business.

My dream for you is that you become a model citizen of whichever society you choose to be in and conduct yourself as an honest, worthy, responsible and productive citizen of that country. No matter how transnational you are or how American (you have been living there from the age of seventeen), you will always be seen as an Indian. Therefore, uphold the image of India in every action of yours.

Be successful. Success to me is bringing a smile to the faces of people when you enter a room. Becoming so requires you to be caring of other people. I know this is your fundamental strength. Put the interest of the society ahead of your own family's interest, and the interest of your family ahead of your own personal interest. That is the only way, my child, that we can make this a better world for our children and grandchildren.

I appreciate your penchant for following the golden rule—Do unto others what you want others to do unto you—to ensure fairness in everything we do. Many times people ask me how I want to be remembered. My answer has always been that I want to be remembered as a fair person, *not a good person. To put yourself in someone's shoes to understand their feelings.'*

There is a joke in our family that the only person I am scared of, who can rein me in, is my daughter. Throughout my career—at the Indian Institute of Management, Ahmedabad, while working in Paris at Patni Computer Systems and finally at Infosys, I really did not have a boss. In the first three places, since I worked hard to deliver whatever I agreed on time, within budget, and with the requisite quality, my bosses left me alone. Since I founded Infosys, I had no boss! So, the only boss I have known is you! Who else can order me around about my eating habits, my sleep patterns, my incessant traveling, and my refusal to go for regular medical check-ups? Rohan is my buddy, but you are the one who instills discipline in my life.

Take care, my child!

Lovingly,
Appa

While this book was under publication, Murthy became grandfather a second time and Akshata is now mother to two little daughters, Krishnaa and Anoushka.

Pradeep Bhargava

Pradeep Bhargava, Director at Cummins India and Chairman of the Confederation of Indian Industry's (CII) Western Region, is a man who believes in doing things differently. In a corporate set-up where top honchos have an abundance of perks and privileges, this was the man who set up a precedent to do as much of his work as possible, by himself. Much to the astonishment and consternation of his staff at Cummins Generator Technologies where he was the Managing Director, he decided to eat in the staff canteen where he served himself and washed his own plates, after keeping the leftover food aside. After each meal, the leftovers in the canteen got weighed and a chart was put up with the total leftover food weighed so that the staff would know the quantity of food wasted every day. The leftover food was then used for vermiculture within the factory. In effect, it was a symbolic message for conservation and also a strong message to his staff about the importance of not wasting food when thousands of children in the world die of starvation.

In a career that has seen him work in the public as well as private sector, with stints also at UNDP and the World Bank, Bhargava has always been steered by an inner calling that saw him rise above the profile of his job to do something for the community around him. The inspiration for this came from his father, a Public Health Engineer with the Rajasthan

Government. Pradeep remembers that spark of joy in his father's eyes every time he was able to do something for the people, such as providing safe drinking water supply to the community. The young boy grew up idolizing his father and his thoughts and in the years since then, he has done his own bit for the community such as helping Pune city, his adopted home, free of the scourge of debilitating load shedding and power outages through a unique private and public sector partnership.

Bhargava is also the brain behind CII's Finishing School project, a unique venture that he started off in collaboration with Pune's Symbiosis College wherein scheduled caste and scheduled tribe students in the third year of engineering colleges got trained in a variety of soft skills and business etiquette in order to develop their personality and make them more employable. 'They already had the required vocational skills; what we did was to make them more confident individuals who could compete with their more urbane, sophisticated city counterparts. These kids had been denied opportunities and put on the back foot for so long that we needed to help them believe that they could do it.' The Finishing College experiment is now being replicated by CII's branches in other parts of the country. Pradeep is also closely involved in the academic world where he has helped educational institutions in their development and curriculum, besides being engaged with Institutes such as TMTC, YASHDA, IIM Ahmedabad, IIM Bangalore, and Symbiosis Institutes, as a visiting faculty.

Now in his retirement phase but with a plateful of

assignments to keep him busy, Bhargava's biggest lesson was learnt nearly two decades ago, when he lay in a pool of blood in his house, after being assaulted by robbers who had broken in. In the days that he spent in the intensive care unit of a hospital, lonely and scared, Bhargava realized the ultimate truth that seems to escape most of us: That we are completely replaceable at our workplaces but there is never a back-up for us at home.

'I did make it to the hospital and pulled through the crisis but in those days of uncertainty and loneliness in the ICU, I realized that the most important thing in my life was my family. I realized that it was not the next promotion or designation that mattered in life. In some ways, perhaps, all these years since then have been a 'bonus' for me, but that episode helped shape what is truly important in life and how we should not get consumed by so many trivialities and pettiness in everyday life,' Bhargava writes to his daughter Pooja, a young professional in an IT firm and mother to a young son.

Dearest Pooja,

It's been a long time since you and I had one of our famous 'man to man' talks, the kind you would nudge me into having during your teenage years when there was something that you needed to share with me. A lot has happened in our lives since then. You found your life partner and are now a young mother. I too got busy in my career and have spent these years fully immersed in my Corporate 'Grahastha' mode and I sometimes wonder if I could have spent more time with my family.

After 40 plus years of an exciting professional career, I'm now moving to my 'Vanaprastha' phase and I think the time is perfect for us to have one of our 'man to mans'. It has been a memorable journey for me, one that started with a career in the public sector, took me to UNDP and World Bank, and finally put me through the hierarchies of the private sector and corporate world in India. But while I continue to carry a corporate visiting card, I have chosen to spend my time and energy on engagements I truly enjoy and am getting used to a retired life where compulsions are few and freedom is high. It is clearly a good time to capture the learning through a bit of 'rewind and replay' and even attempt to 'fast forward' to what could be a fulfilling direction for the remaining days of my life. And who can be a better person than you to share my journey and learning with!

Dear bitiya, to begin with, I would like to tell you something that is on top of my mind, always. I know you have heard this before but I still would love to tell you this: You and your brother Amit have been the best things that have happened to us—your mother and I. All the designations and achievements in my career pale into insignificance when compared to the joy I experience when I see you both now, grown up into splendid people with courage and conviction of your own.

As I rewind, I would like to first capture the learning

on the professional front. And possibly try and answer the question all of us ask ourselves in our introspective moments: 'If I were to start my life once again, would I steer it differently?'

Pooja, all of us base our lives on that one person who inspires you so much that you want to follow in his or her footsteps. My idol was my father. Such was his impact on my mind that even after passing out of the prestigious IIM, Ahmedabad with a gold medal, when I could have had a picking of the best jobs around, I chose to work with Bharat Sarkar and continued doing that for eleven long years. My father spent his entire working life with the Government of Rajasthan where, as Chief Engineer of the Public Health Engineering Department, he made a huge difference in the lives of people. I grew up seeing the twinkle in his eyes when he steered schemes to provide drinking water to people in the parched desert state. What joy and fulfilment! I had the same zeal and dream. And honestly, if I were to graduate from IIM, Ahmedabad today and if there was an iconic and charming leader like Dr Vikram Sarabhai, who recruited many of us in 1971 from IIM, Ahmedabad, into Atomic Energy and Space Research Organizations, I would still opt to work for him and the cause. It was all about doing something on a larger societal canvas, and I then felt that it would be easier if I were to work for State enterprise. It was only after life started unfolding, that I realized that you don't necessarily have to be a 'public-servant' for serving a public cause. But the experience and exposure of the public sector was valuable and extremely useful when I entered the public space later in life while working for private enterprises. How can it not have? I have had the privilege and opportunity of working with some of the country's tallest visionaries such as Dr Vikram Sarabhai and Prof MGK Menon who made a big difference in my professional upbringing and values.

A decade later, I entered the private sector and have spent the last 27 years as Managing Director in some of the country's well-known corporate houses (Kalyani-Sharp, General Electric, and now Cummins India), gaining a span of expertize in setting up and running companies, mergers, acquisitions...in a variety of markets and sectors ranging from industrial to consumer goods, both for domestic and international business. But you know that your father was no 'race horse' and has had his share of discomfort being on the race track. But in some ways, I have to acknowledge that my designations and empowering superiors gave me the opportunity of serving common cause by pulling 'tongas' in public life. These regular detours onto the side roads were my greatest joys while I was driving on the corporate expressway.

The urge of going beyond corporate expectations and roles was always there in some corner of my heart and it drove me to take up activities that brought me closer to civic society. It came not from any disenchantment with corporate life but from a positive desire to go beyond. Honestly, I thoroughly enjoyed my corporate role—its passion and pressures, highs and lows, adrenalin of growth and pains of decline, creating jobs and wealth, and engaging in its own contribution to society and environment. The Confederation of Indian Industry (CII) was an excellent platform which gave me an opportunity to deliver and seek fulfilment from a space which individual corporates normally don't focus on. CII has been the best enabler for me, and I learnt so much through my association with some outstanding and caring corporate leaders in this country.

Gudiya, let me start by sharing a journey which has made a deep impact on my persona and in the lives of lakhs of fellow beings around us. Almost a decade ago, Pune city, which had been our home for many years, started experiencing crippling power shortage (affecting the entire State of Maharashtra) resulting in extended load shedding every day. I remember the public outrage when the state government threw up its hands and said the power shortages would continue for the next few years. It struck me then that instead of whining or blaming the government, all of us had the choice of taking control of the situation and resolving the problem. I took upon myself what everyone considered the unrealistic responsibility of making the city of Pune free of load shedding. It was a formidable task considering that I had no framework to work upon and the government had nothing to offer. On the CII platform, we worked on a unique and innovative solution by which industrial units in the city cooperated and used their captive gensets for their needs during peak hours, thereby releasing grid capacity for the citizens who then did not have load shedding. A new framework involving Regulator, State Utility Company, Government, Industry, NGOs and consumers was evolved. Details are not important here, but after three years of stubborn struggle, the city of Pune became load shedding free on 6 June, 2006 and has stayed so since then. It was almost a miracle and it was done not by dependence on the State but by a citizen-industry movement. We have to go beyond analysing problems and offering advice...we need to be a part of the solution. The e-mails and calls I still get from unknown faces and names, thanking me for resolving a daily pain in their lives, are the best reward I can ever aspire for. For me, it was also reiteration of the belief that it is possible for each one of us to bring positive change with commitment and persistence.

In our family, all of us know the value of the words commitment and persistence, don't we? How can we not? It is these two qualities alone that brought back your brother Amit from the months that he was bedridden after the medical set back eleven years ago. Amit was so young and full of life and so much involved in his passion for tennis and a variety of other sports. I've never been able to forget the shock and the searing pain that went through me when I saw my young son on that hospital bed and the doctor's words that it would be a long haul to recovery. We were all devastated, and for you it was even worse because he was your confidant and soul mate. All of us marvel at Amit's tremendous will power, his insistence on appearing for his engineering finals with a writer to help him, his moment of triumph when he cleared it with a distinction, and his every triumph since then. After that episode, the 'fittest boy in town became the strongest boy in town.' In all the years since, Amit leads a full life and has a great career. One can only salute the human spirit when we see Amit with his loving wife Minu and their angel of a daughter, Suhani.

Pooja, through it all, your mother and I remember how generously you gave of yourself to your brother. At 24, you had a promising career and life but you put your every pre-occupation aside to immerse yourself in getting your brother back on his feet, completely recovered. The love, care, dedication that you gave was not only heart-warming, but one of the key factors that contributed to his recovery. For us as a family, it was a period of bonding, committing ourselves to each other and learning about the power of a positive attitude and persistence.

Like in my personal life, I have always encouraged the corporate sector to commit themselves to the welfare of the community around them. The success of my Pune Power Model and its replication in other cities is validation of my faith that clarity of goals, honesty of purpose, and perseverance will always pay off.

Dear Pooja, other things in my life have also shaped the person I am today, a silent activist. As a child and later, when I was in school, I would be mystified by my grandparents and their queries about the surnames of my friends who came visiting at our home in Rajasthan. I would sometimes dismiss it as harmless curiosity and at other times as an annoying habit. It was only years later that I realized the shameful secret behind their questions: it was the hideous classification of people based on their castes!

Over my years in corporate life, I have seen how young men and women from certain sections of society, castes and tribes struggle to find their own place in the larger society *around them. They come from disadvantaged economic and social backgrounds but strive hard to improve their lives. But years, indeed, generations of discrimination have rendered them at a disadvantage when competing with the world around them. Often, they have to do jobs much below their actual qualifications and abilities and somewhere the realization came to me that we need to do prayashchit (penance) for the paap (sins) of our forefathers. I am neither a social reformer, nor a politician but I was convinced that I could play a role in giving those children from socially challenged sections an opportunity to unleash their full potential and lead a life of self-respect. I knew what these young people lack is a huge boost in self-confidence and self-belief. The inability to communicate or articulate their point with the suaveness of us city-bred people and a lack of grooming have also combined to keep them away from the plum positions that could be theirs, given their skill sets. I had a vision in my mind, of giving them a fair chance in life and it got translated into the now famous 'Finishing School' for students from the scheduled castes and tribes, a concept wherein we impart a clutch of soft skills so that these young people emerge as strong candidates for employment, employability, and entrepreneurship. This powerful affirmative action, made possible by the collaboration between CII and the Symbiosis educational institutes, has changed the lives of hundreds of students over the years and has since then been replicated at many locations and covers a wide variety of vocations ranging from ITI's, Polytechnics, Engineering, and even MBA students.*

A few months ago, I was rushing to check into my hotel room before heading out to a conference when the young woman at the reception surprised me by thanking for transforming her life. Taken aback, I excused myself saying I could not recall if we had met before. She smiled brightly, telling me that she had passed out of one of our Finishing School batches and had been selected for a job on the basis of merit, almost immediately after that. She had always aspired to work at a five-star hotel and the soft skills she had learnt gave her the confidence to show her talent. Pooja, I cannot express the satisfaction and joy that I derived from that young woman's story. I had managed to use my position as a corporate leader and CII office bearer to create a platform, influence a cross section of industry leaders and education institutions, to benefit the section of society which has been traditionally neglected. Without politicizing anything or discussing quotas and abilities, I had managed to alleviate a long-standing scourge of society. God creates everybody equal and does not give IQs to children on the basis of their surname. We give surnames later and create stigmas. Every child is entitled to fair opportunity and I know this movement that I initiated will make a difference in many lives.

I am asked by my many friends why I have not opted to be a full time activist—a social crusader or even get into active politics. My answer is a question—'For Bhakti (devotion to God), does one have to be a priest or go to a temple?' Each one of us can do it from where we are; if we really care. May be I did not have the courage to fully give up my comfort zone but the important thing was to listen to my heart and doing what gives me joy.

Some of my friends in the corporate world often tell me about their plans to devote a lot of their time and resources to social agenda later in life, after they have achieved their professional goals, settled their children etc. etc... My advice to them, always, is that the process of 'settling' never happens in life and our social commitments have to be honoured in everyday life. Unfortunately, many of us consider the obligations to society as an option to be exercised if and when it suits us. Very often we get so engrossed in our personal lives that we forget that there is a larger world outside of our small families and that each one of us owes something to this other world. Much as I was engaged in undoing (in a limited manner) the wrongs of our caste system, I got drawn into yet another engagement, this time, with the environment.

Over the last few years, I have been preoccupied with the thought that just as our purvajs (forefathers) left the wrong legacy of the caste system in our society, the present generation will, if its reckless behaviour is not checked, leave a depleted and dangerous planet for the next generation. And we have no right to do this under the garb of development. Like many others, I am convinced that Vikas does not have to lead to Vinash (Development can coexist with Environment Sanity). That is how I started my Green journey and set up the country's first Green Factory, near Pune. It was a fascinating search for harmony which not only transformed the approach to development but has become the guiding

164

light for many organizations in the country. My employer Cummins, which strongly supported my initiative, has made this project part of its best practice, worldwide. What has emerged is the amazing business case for Green. I keep reminding everyone that it is no longer nice to be Green but you are dumb if you are not Green. From the success of this green factory building, I am now driving through CII, a national movement towards 'Green Companies', wherein organizations move towards a wholesome , environmentally sensitive conduct in all its functioning. Once again, a detour Pooja, for an agenda that affected society; but done within the contours and context of the corporate world. It further reinforced my conviction that societal agenda can be addressed from different platforms and is certainly not the exclusive domain of either the State or social and political organizations. You can be an activist in the Boardroom and nobody needs to take a sabbatical to address issues of People and Planet.

Often our personal values also become the values that we mimic at our workplaces. Throughout my growing up years, I saw the love and admiration that my father got from the organization that he worked for. Government jobs are often thankless and offer limited rewards to individuals. And yet, my father was a much-loved, respected, and admired man. Looking back, I know that it was from the way he brought grace, dignity, and the quality of caring in his job. It is from him that I adopted my own equation with the people around me, at work, in the community and in the family. When times are bad, corporates often have a propensity to try and rectify the situation by getting rid of the people. Many years ago, in the midst of a crucial acquisition and merger, I remember my boss gave me a clear brief to 'change' people, especially at the leadership level, so that the integration of the companies could happen quickly and seamlessly. A year later, I had delivered the desired result of integration with outstanding success. But my boss realized that I had not got rid of the people at the leadership level as he had expected and directed. He questioned me and I responded by pointing out that I had, in fact, 'changed' people—but by bringing changes in them with respect to organization culture / processes etc. It goes back to care and grace. Pooja, these attributes are like our health—you realize its importance when it fails you. Each one of us experiences joys and pangs, excitement and breakdowns, preferences and prejudices and above all surprises when we are least prepared for it. But what we recall the most with extreme emotions are instances when we were treated with care or when grace and dignity was dispensed with. Increments and promotion as occasions are important but they fade with time. The enduring images in our hearts are that of kindness and grace and friendship from unexpected quarters.

It is said our various life experiences shape us and make us the people we are. Certainly, these societal detours made me a more sensitive, caring, and knowledgeable leader at work. Equally important, it made me emotionally and mentally less vulnerable to ups and downs of corporate life. There was always something exciting happening in my life which prepared me to handle business cycles with lesser pressure. People often ask me how I get the energy to do all these things while still delivering full corporate responsibility. Frankly, these activities don't consume my energy—they give me energy!

Gudiya, each one of us choose a path to follow in our lives. For some it is achieving greater heights of corporate ladder and fulfilment at work. Others take up academics and yet others, sports. I chose to take up detours into socially useful projects, while still at work. That was my attempt at actualization. There is never a correct mix applicable to all. Each one can and does choose a recipe for life. My own life recipe changed during the long, lonely days that I spent in the intensive care unit of Bombay Hospital, some twenty years ago, after being grievously injured in a tussle with robbers who had broken into our home in the dead of the night. Even today, I break out in sweat when I think of the concern and the anger that coursed through me when I realized that there were robbers in the house and that they might harm my little children sleeping in the next room. I rushed out and grappled with them, trying to keep them from getting anywhere near both of you but ended up getting brutally assaulted. Pooja, even in the midst of that danger, my only thought was my children's safety, and I recall how you stood terror-stricken, at the sight of me lying in a pool of blood, on the floor. I did make it to the hospital and pulled through the crisis but in those days of uncertainty and loneliness in the ICU, I realized that the most important thing in my life was my family. I realised that it was not the next promotion or designation that mattered in life. In *some ways, perhaps, all these years since then have been a bonus for me, but that episode helped me shape what is truly important in life and how we should not get consumed by so many trivialities and pettiness in everyday life .Faced with the uncertainty of life and certainty of death, I have shaped my life by scripting in my head the 'obituary' that I would like to have for myself. With that script it becomes so much easier to make choices in life.*

Like every professional going through the 'rough and fun' journey, I had choices to make but in my head, since that harrowing time in our lives, there has never been any confusion on the priority between family and work. I have often shared this with my colleagues when they seek permission or time off for something important at home: In our work environment, we have succession planning and role sharing ; at home there are no 'backfills'. Work does go on in our absence (and sometimes that humbles us); but there is no substitute for us, at home. Important events and occasions in your personal life never come back but at work, you can make a difference in the next quarter or close the next deal. Which is why, I often made those really long detours for two-day visits to USA when your little Sahil was a tiny tot. My friends and yours too, commented on the strangeness of a detour to USA when I was actually meant to do London-Mumbai, but I would not have missed seeing him take his first steps or mouthing his first words, for anything in the world. For me, spending time with my children ,three wonderful grandchildren and their lovely spouses Minu and Aseem, is not about work-life balance...it is about LIFE itself; not to be confused with what we do for a 'living!' What matters in the end for all of us is the lasting impression that we leave behind. Was he a caring, nurturing, humble human being? Did he leave a legacy of honesty, sincerity and love behind him? That is what matters…

For me retirement has not brought the slowing down that it brings along for most people. I continue to work as hard, only this time it is with projects that I enjoy taking up, the ones that make a difference to the people around me. I am engaging myself with many educational institutions like IIMs, Symbiosis, not only for teaching but in the journey of institution-building. I have intimate relationship with NGOs and of course steer so many CII initiatives. It means the world to me that my Pune Power Model and Green Factory experiment are case studies used at IIM Bangalore and Ahmedabad respectively. And even though I still have long hours and endless things to do, I know that at the end of the day, I get to unwind in the company of my grandchildren and that is enough to take away the fatigue.

Pooja, when I see you head to the school bus stop every morning, holding Diya's little hand, I remember taking you to the school bus stop in Delhi thirty years ago. When I see Sahil on the tennis court for coaching, I can almost see Amit in him so many years ago. If growing old gives you an opportunity to see your children in your grandchildren, I would have welcomed it much earlier. One of the biggest joys of our life has been seeing both of your grow up with good, home grown sanskars. The credit for the wholesome upbringing goes to your mother, who, without any hesitation, gave up her career as an architect, to focus on you both. Her efforts have more than paid off—and we can see her magic work with her grandchildren.

I want to close this letter with the fun question we all used to chuckle about as you kids were growing up—how did God choose to send the best son and best daughter in the world to the same parents. Gudiya, I am still posing the same question to God and am grateful to him for his kindness.

Lots of love and blessings,
Papa

Prakash Padukone

Meeting Prakash Padukone was in some way a dream come true for me, the one rare occasion when I was completely tongue-tied and at a loss for words. I still remember that school-going girl that I was then, sitting on the edge of the sofa in our drawing room, with my badminton-loving father seated beside me. I was too young to know the intricacies of the game but was used to hitting the shuttle around, with my father on the other side of the net, during our summer holidays in my home town, Kerala.

Back then, even if I did not know the rules of the game, I remember being struck by the intensity on face of the striking young man on television and his dogged determination to get the better of his rival on the other side. I can't even recall the names of the tournaments that he participated in but I do remember watching several of them, each of which got wildly applauded not just by my father and me but by the entire country. India did not have multiple television channels back in the late seventies. In fact, there was just one dedicated to sports and we got to largely watch cricket, hockey, or badminton, the last of which this young man had brought into the limelight with his brilliance. Along the way, the young man became a formidable force in the global badminton arena, snapping up trophies and awards from all corners of the world and bringing to an end the domination of the Chinese players in the game.

The soft-spoken gentleman who offered me tea at his old-world office at the Tata Padukone Badminton Academy was reluctant to talk about his achievements but happily talked about his journey to the top of the pile, in the game. He recounted for me the years spent practicing the game at a small wedding hall in Malleswaram, Bangalore, where he would wait anxiously for the marriage season to end so that he and his cronies could hone their game. Even today he credits his father for his success and for giving him the wings to fly. At a time when middle-class parents hoped for their sons to become doctors or engineers so that they could look after their families, Ramesh Padukone let his son follow his dream of achieving greatness in Badminton, a game which was little known in India and in which a top award was usually a wooden plaque.

The young man did achieve his dream when he won the All England Badminton Championship in 1980, vanquishing one of the game's most revered figures, Indonesia's Liem Swie King in straight sets, putting his country on the badminton map of the world. Suddenly, India was a force to reckon with in this sport. The Gentle Giant of the court got a new name, 'Bangalore Torpedo', an icon who destroyed the world's greatest players with a combination of deceptive but deadly wristwork, an uncanny ability to read his opponents, a much-feared 'Net dribble', and delicate drop shots. When he could not combat the aggressive physical smashes, he simply decided he would play his opponents on the mind level, bringing them down with strategy rather than physical strength.

India welcomed its sporting hero with the kind of celebration it had never before laid down—fans thronged the fifteen kilometre route from the airport to his house, raining flowers on the shy young lad, who, with this victory, made badminton a sport that was suddenly as popular as cricket or hockey.

What he remembers of those years is his middle-class father's great generosity in allowing him to pursue a sport that had little money or prospects, his refusal to crib about his circumstances, and the all-encompassing passion for the game that gave him the strength to take on the countless trips made in unreserved compartments of trains, sleeping on the floor, or spending nights on railway platforms so that he could get to his destination and play a good tournament.

When he hung up his boots, retiring after he had given his everything to the game, Padukone set up the eponymous Prakash Padukone Badminton Academy in Bangalore, where he spends his days training the badminton heroes of the future. Along with billiards champion Geet Sethi, he also founded Olympics Gold Quest—a voluntary body that spots and funds India's best prospective gold medal winners for the Olympic games. 'It is only when each of us contribute in whatever capacity we can, no matter how small or big the amount, that we can fund our poor but immensely talented athletes. They have the fire in the belly to want to win the ultimate honor for our country but sadly, they don't have the wherewithal to fund the long journey and tough training that it takes to compete with the world's best', he says.

The master badminton players writes a letter to his daughters, film actor Deepika Padukone, and golfer Anisha, making a strong case for keeping their feet on the ground, eyes focused on their goals, and quietly going about their work with single-minded devotion.

❧

Dear Deepika, Anisha,

As you stand on the threshold of life's journey, I want to share with you some lessons that life has taught me.

Decades ago, as a little boy growing up in Bangalore, I started my tryst with badminton, a game that was completely unknown in our country at the time, except in some parts of West and North India. My father, your grandfather Ramesh Padukone, had become fascinated by the game when he lived in Mumbai and introduced it in Bangalore when he relocated there. He took a group of us, young boys, under his wings to teach us the basics, often looking up rule books so that he could impart to us the finer nuances of the game.

Those days there were no stadiums and courts where sportspeople could train without being disturbed. Our badminton court was the marriage hall of the Canara Union bank, near our house in Malleswaram, and it was there that I learnt everything about the game.

Every day, we would wait to see if there was a function

in the hall, and if there was none, we would rush there, after school, to play to our hearts' content. Marriage season in Bangalore often lasted for five to six months and so there were not too many days we could play at a stretch. Sometimes, it would be just nine to ten days in a month, but we were grateful for even those days.

Looking back, I realize that the most important thing about my childhood and adolescent years was my refusal to complain about my lot in life. I was thankful for the few hours a week we had the opportunity to hit the shuttle back and forth.

In fact, that has possibly been the foundation on which I based my career and my life—the refusal to whinge or whine about anything, even as a child of seven when I first took up the game.

I could have complained about everything—the lack of proper sparring partners, the shortage of practice matches, the unavailability of coaches and fitness trainers, poor infrastructure for training, and so on. But I, in fact a generation of people in the seventies, chose to just accept the conditions that we were presented with and made the best out of them.

And that is what I want to tell you my children, that there is no substitute for perseverance, hard work, determination, and passion for what you choose to do. If you love what you do, nothing else matters—not awards, nor compensation, not even the gratification of seeing your face in newspapers or television.

By the time I was sixteen, I was the national badminton

champion. Often the prize for the effort was a candle-stand, a photo-frame, or a wooden plaque.

It was only when I won the All England Championship that the prize-money became significant—£3,000—a huge amount in those days. But that did not distract me from the sheer joy of having been instrumental in putting India on the global map of this game.

In a small way, I think, my winning that championship was the turning point for the game in India and it cleared the way for other champions to come in later.

The success, the name and fame, the Arjuna Award and Padma Shri, were all by-products of my love for the game.

Deepika, we know that you are in the film industry because of your love for it. Early on in life, even as a child of nine or ten, we knew that you were meant for modelling and to be under the arc-lights. You were a natural.

Even so, at eighteen, when you told us that you wanted to shift to Mumbai to pursue a career in modelling, it was hard for us to come to terms with the decision. We felt you were too young and too inexperienced to be alone in a big city, in an industry we knew nothing about.

In the end we decided to let you follow your heart, like my father had taught me all those years ago, as the only way to live fully.

In the sixties, most middle-class families had their sons into engineering or medicine as that guaranteed a secure and stable future. Your uncle, Pradeep, and I were Junior National Champions together, but he pursued his interest *in engineering and went off to the US for a career. I, on the other hand, had no intention of going down that path, and I was fortunate that my father gave me the freedom to follow my passion for a game which held very little promise of ever making money. His approval changed the course of my life. Had he forced me, I would have been a miserable, average engineer plodding through life.*

When the time came for you to make a decision about your future, we thought it would be cruel to not give our child the opportunity to pursue a dream that she lived and breathed for. If you succeeded, it would make us proud, but even if you didn't, you would not have any regrets that you did not try. In retrospect, it has turned out to be the best thing we did.

In the last few years, we have seen you mature into a young woman who has her head on her shoulders. Maybe it is a result of the responsibilities that came your way at an early age, but we are proud of the independent, sensible, focused young woman that you have become, a woman who effortlessly manages the things that compete for her attention every day—a demanding career, keeping house, managing the staff, and keeping in touch with family.

Sometimes parents underestimate their children's capabilities which brings me to my other belief: you can either like what you do or you can be passionate about what you do. If you only like what you do, you will become an average player, but if you love what you do, there is every chance that you will excel at it. For then, no hardship, no sacrifice will be too much to achieve your goal. Anisha, you want to be a professional golfer and I know you will let nothing come between you and that dream.

At sixteen years of age, when I was representing the country in badminton, I travelled second class and often in unreserved coaches on trains, sitting, eating, and sleeping outside filthy toilets in the train for a couple of days simply so that I could reach the training camp and better my game. I see that passion in you. I don't know too many young people who work sixteen hours a day and I see that the fruits of that passion are already coming your way.

Deepika, I have learned that you can't always win in life, that everything you want might not come your way, and events don't always turn out as you want them to. To win some, you have to lose some. You have to learn to take life's ups and downs in your stride. Looking back, the amount of effort that I put in my game never varied from the first day till my retirement, regardless of the money, the awards and recognition, winning or losing. Whatever I got in addition to playing was just added bonus.

Even during the toughest times, I focused on what I had, instead of dwelling on what I did not. I had the ability to make the best of the worst circumstances and remain steadfast to my goal. Thus, at the end of my career, I had no regrets, or any desire to ever return to the game, for I knew that I had truly given all to my passion.

Remember how I constantly tell you both about the importance of making your way up in the world without waiting for your parents to pull strings and make things happen for you? I believe it is best for children to work hard to make their dreams come true and to not have things handed to them on a platter. And it makes us immensely proud to see that both of you have followed our counsel and are making things happen for yourself.

When you are home visiting us, Deepika, you make your own bed, clear the table after meals, and sleep on the floor if there are guests at home. At home, you are not a star, and that is because we have taught you to be rooted in reality at all times. Showbiz is about make-believe. Everybody will rush to do things for you and pander to your every desire when you are on top. But the cameras that follow you everywhere will eventually fade and what will remain is the real world. If you occasionally wonder why we refuse to treat you like a star, it is because you are our daughter first and a film star later, and we want you to remember that you have to eventually return to the real world.

Dear Deepika, you are in an industry where there is much negativity, but I hope that you are the game-changer in it. As in every other industry, so too here, there is a place for everyone, and I believe that you don't have to put anyone down in order to get work. If you can live your life without harming anyone, or talking badly about anyone, you can set an example for others. You might not succeed, you might even risk ridicule, yet continue to refuse to be a part of the circle of negativity. Strive to generate positivity around you even though you are too new and too small a player to effect a big change. Often you will find people who will lie and say untruths about you, but remember never to retaliate or talk their language. If what they say is untrue, ignore it. And if it is true, use their criticism to improve and transform yourself.

You are in an industry where there's always going to be big money, but I hope that's not your only motivation for work. I believe that it is important to try to be the best in whatever you do, regardless of money. Always focus on what you want to become as an individual and empower yourself to reach your goals without distractions. That big car or 'things' will follow later.

The things that really matter in life are relationships, honesty, and respect for your parents, and elders. Material success is important, not fundamental to happiness and peace of mind.

I have not always been perfect, but over the years I have learnt to strike a balanced view of life. After a life well lived, what is important to me today is peace of mind and good health. Your health is your most important wealth. Take care of it, nurture it.

I can't tell you enough about the rejuvenating power of prayers and a little faith. You know it, of course, because offering prayers is a long-standing tradition in our family. Now that you are a professional with a demanding career, you might not always find the time to accompany us on our annual pilgrimage to Tirupati. Instead, spare a few minutes of your day, even if it is just twenty, to close your eyes and meditate, to think about God and you will see how much that faith in His power will strengthen you.

In the end, when your career is behind you, what remains

with you and for you is family, the friends that you have made who will stand by you.

Live a life that is healthy, my children, and one that will allow you to live with your own conscience. Everything else is transient. And remember, no matter what, we are always going to be there for you.

Lovingly,
Papa

P.P. Chhabria

P.P. Chhabria was born in pre-independence Karachi into a wealthy trading family that raised its children with immense luxury. Pahlaj, (as he was fondly called) and his nine siblings grew up in a sprawling bungalow set amid lush gardens and towering trees. He still remembers the happy times when the kids would go off on jaunts in horse carriages that were specially maintained for them, with dedicated staff to supervize.

But that life of comforts soon changed into a nightmare when his father died unexpectedly of a massive heart attack, leaving behind a grieving wife and young children. Almost immediately afterwards, his elder siblings speculated, unwisely as it turned out, in the commodities market and had to sell the family assets to repay creditors. And yet, he says, his mother, a hardworking woman who slogged silently to tend to her family, never complained because she knew her boys had to sell the family assets to honour their father's name.

Twelve-year-old Pahlaj was put to work in a small wholesale cloth merchant's shop, working as a lowly paid worker sweeping and cleaning, doing odd jobs around the place and offering tea and refreshments to the people who came there to tie up business deals. For the young man who had been used to having a paid servant to bathe and dress him, this came as a huge blow and proved to be a humiliation which he says had him raging against destiny.

The tough years continued, with one menial job after the other, till his family packed him off to faraway Poona to work as a servant in his paternal aunt's home for a monthly salary of Rs 30 and lodging.

Looking back at his life on a high summer Pune afternoon last year, PP saab, as he is fondly called in his adopted city where his stature now is that of a loved family elder, told me it was his deep longing to free himself from the life of indignity and bondage that led him on a journey that began as a small time salesman of electrical accessories to the head of a Rs 4,000 crore plus conglomerate.

'It has been a journey of great learning,' said the 82-year-old patriarch of the Finolex group of industries, who continues to lead a life of discipline and hard work, despite the fact that the younger generation has stepped in to look after the business. Being a salesman who hopped from one tiny shop to the other in the tiny town of Pune taught him to be patient, determined, and persistent. If a shopkeeper refused to entertain him on his first five visits and shooed him away, he would go away silently and return a few days later, to make his sales pitch. And, if a buyer refused to keep his word and pay him, he continued to turn up at the shop, politely asking for the payment till the recalcitrant buyer dipped into his pocket and repaid his dues!

The journey from being an electrical switches and ceiling roses salesman to a businessman trading electrical cables and wires led him to become a defense and government supplier. At each stage, the confidence that he got led him to eventually set up his own cable manufacturing business, Finolex Cables, in 1958. The Finolex group of companies today boasts of multiple companies and eleven modern manufacturing facilities across the country. It has won several national and international awards and has been acknowledged as one of the country's most quality conscious groups and wealth creators. It also has the distinct honour of being the number one manufacturer of cables in the country.

Such an arduous journey to the top of the charts has taught him about the value of being kind and cordial to people, because his own life was built brick by brick on the foundation of unexpected kindness of other people, some strangers, some even more poor than him.

Which is why, to this day, he makes it a point to make time for the humblest of his staff on the shop floor, stopping to listen to and sometimes take feedback from the watchman or the peon who have devoted decades of their lives in his service. It is a matter of great pride to him that the children of some of these loyal workers now hold positions in his group.

His one regret in life continues to be the fact that he never went to school after the age of 12. It was the fact that he was unlettered that relegated him to menial jobs for a large part of his life and while he painstakingly taught himself to speak and write in English, one of the requirements for his job as a door to door salesman, he continues to regret that he could not complete his formal education.

The Interntational Institute for Information Technology (IIIT), Pune, an educational institution that he set up in

Pune, now run by his only daughter, Aruna, stands testimony to his belief in the redeeming power of education. IIIT has grown to be a widely respected institution of learning for cutting-edge developments in Information Technology and other high-tech areas.

My own memories of PP saab go back to the early nineties when I would run into him and his walking group at the thickly wooded, colonial era campus of the University of Pune. I was a struggling young mother trying to balance the competing demands of a toddler and a cherished career as a journalist. Early every morning I would head for a walk in the magnificent woods of the university campus. That was the one hour in the day that belonged to me, when I could regain my calm by breathing in the fresh morning air with the sounds of birds humming. Sometimes I would run into PP and would exchange pleasantries with him. On a few occasions we found ourselves heading towards the University at the same time so I would walk with him, often having to almost run to keep up with his fast pace and we would exchange notes about life and work.

At 82, PP continues to live and work with a discipline that few of us can match. He continues to remain true to his morning walks.

'All my life, I have followed the practice of waking early, working all day and sleeping early. To wake early is to experience a freshness of the spirit. When you walk alone in the fresh morning air, nature walks with you and speaks to you, bringing ideas, energy, and the courage to make quick decisions. My association with the sky continues to fuel me with the power to envision and strive.'

(Taken from his autobiography,
There's No Such Thing as a Self-made Man.)

Here, he writes a touching, surprisingly candid, and infinitely wise letter to his daughter Aruna Katara, herself a mother of two today. Aruna steers the growth of IIIT, her once-upon-a-time-unlettered father's ode to the benefits of formal education.

Dear Aruna,

I know this is letter that has been long in writing, a letter that I should have actually sent you years ago when you were a young girl growing up with dreams, hopes, and aspirations. You are a mature woman now but I want you to know that this has been a letter I have been writing to you in my mind for many, many years. And, like they say, it is never too late for anything. I know the best years of your life are yet to come and I can see from the way you lead your life now that your dreams are about to take flight.

Aruna, I don't know if I have told you this before but through this letter, I want to tell you how precious a gift you were to your mother and me from the day you were born. You were a kind, gentle, studious little child who quietly bore being left alone to grow on her own when your mother and I focused on your sister as she struggled with a fatal illness. Not once in all those years that we paid little heed to you and your brother, did you complain or rebel against our continued absence from your life. Your sister passed away and when we recovered from our grief, you had already become a self-sustained person who had learnt to live life on her own.

Dear child, looking back today, I confess I never realized when and how you grew up. Back then, I was still a struggling entrepreneur trying to grow his business and life was an endless journey from small town to yet another small town, in dirty, dusty buses and trains. Money was scarce and making a phone call to my family back home was a needless, unaffordable luxury. It was your mother who shouldered the responsibility of raising both of you since I was never around for either parent-teacher meetings or sports days. Looking back, I think I lost out on a large part of my own life by being detached from your growing up years. But that is life and I always believed in taking each day as it came.

When you came to be of a marriageable age, I decided I did not want you to be wife to a businessman and become like the other women in our traditional community who stayed at home being good wives and mothers, doing little other than attending parties. When we found you a professional doctor as a spouse, it was a happy occasion for us because we knew he would support you in anything that you wanted to do for yourself. For years after that, you raised your kids and looked after your family but I was consumed with the need to leave behind me a legacy that you could take up and run with.

Since I never went to school, I thought why not do something in the field of education and thus was born our first engineering college in Ratnagiri, a project which benefitted the simple people from our beautiful Konkan coast who did not have an engineering college in their region. That fledgling effort has now become a college that is much appreciated and has under its wings as many as four thousand students. But even though you were involved in it from the very beginning, the distance from your home in Pune to Ratnagiri always meant you were not able to work hands-on in the project.

In our families, girls marry young and don the role of traditional housewives. That was precisely the reason why I wanted you to get married to a professional instead of someone from a business family so you could have the option of doing something that would fulfill you, even after marriage. After the engineering college came about, you decided to take its reigns and started the journey of your own life. Later, my meetings with Dr Raghunath Mashelkar and Dr Vijay Bhatkar, (Dr. Mashekar is the former Director General of the Council of Scientific & Industrial Research, Dr. Vijay Bhatkar is one of the key scientists behind India's national initiative in supercomputing , leading the development of Param supercomputers) got me thinking about setting up a path-breaking institute that would provide global quality education in advanced technologies, at affordable prices, to middle-class Indian students who could not afford to pay the exorbitant fees required for foreign education. That, I decided, would be my legacy for you.

In 2000, when I started this project, you took charge of it fully and it remains your passion a decade later. It amazes me how much time and commitment you invest in this project. Now that your children are all grown up, this is your main preoccupation. I'm happy that I have given you something that will outlive me and remain with you for a long time.

Aruna, it makes me happy that you have committed yourself to this institution because it is important to leave something in this world through which you will be remembered. I want you to create a name for yourself, support the poor, and the middle-class. The privileged have their money and their connections but the lesser privileged need the support and guidance of those who have much in their lives.

Through the course of the ten years since the institute's establishment, IIIT has entered into so many joint ventures with foreign institutions. It filled me with pride when you travelled recently to China to work on an invitation by the University of Hunan which wants you to set up a branch of our college in that country. I am proud of you in a way I am not able to express. I grew up a poor, unlettered man and it makes me proud to see you so immersed in a career that has the power to change people's lives.

For a long time after you got married and had children, I struggled to figure out what I could leave you as a legacy. In our community, women don't study enough and often spend time in parties and other equally inconsequential stuff, *but that does not help leaving any legacy. I wanted you to focus on something meaningful that will help the community around you and you have done such a splendid job, Aruna, and created your own identity with it.*

It gives me satisfaction that I have done my job in giving you a meaningful path to follow. I deprived myself of education as a young boy but I wanted you to study and also open that magical door for others.

Aruna, my years on this earth have taught me that the most important thing in life is to never forget your roots, the place you came from before you became rich and successful. The initial years of my life were spent in luxury, but when my father passed away, all the money disappeared and the family came face to face with abject poverty. You know I have done every job from being a cleaning boy in a tiny textile shop in Karachi, to a domestic servant, to being a collection agent before I set up this business which has given me immense wealth and respect. I never let myself forget where I came from and in my daily life at home and at work, I always make time to meet the poor and the underprivileged people around me because that keeps me rooted and reminds me of my difficult initial years.

As you progress in life and move from success to success, be sensitive to the people around you. Ours is a country of vast inequities, so use your money to benefit many. Ultimately when you depart from this earth, you cannot carry your riches and possessions with you. Ashes to ashes, we go back into the earth that we came from. Instead, leave something for society to remember you by.

Because I grew up virtually with no education, I learnt that education is the best way to improve your situation in life and pull yourself out of you poverty and so, setting up a clutch of educational institutions is my way of giving back to society.

Whatever work you are doing, keep thinking ahead of your trade or business or chosen calling. Learning is an endless journey. Have a vision, continually dream new things for yourself, build a body of work, never put limitations on yourself by being timid, never think that you are poor and can't achieve anything. All of us came to this earth with nothing. Establish your credentials with hard work and commitment. Being poor can often be an advantage because it acts as an incentive for you to work hard and excel. And, if you have been blessed by God's grace and have a good life, be humble and aware of the difficulties of people around you.

Aruna, unlike the earlier times in which you grew up, the younger generation is more independent. Let your children be free, be aware of the changes of society around you. The young have their own way of life, don't interfere with it. Our cherished joint family system is gone and it is the best to accept things as they are. I have adopted silence as the best way for myself, leaving the young to find their own way, but I want you to be willing enough to give guidance and advice when your young ones want it.

While you were growing up, I never got the time to instill values in you but I know that if you are attached to your children, they see you and follow your actions and there is no need to teach them anything. Children follow and adopt the things they see around them, so show them by your own living what the right path is.

I admire your hard work, commitment, and complete involvement in managing the growth of an institution that is now already being counted as one of the most forward-looking in the country. You have made it the only organization in the state to get triple IT status (Indian Institute of Information Technology.) When we started, I never imagined that we would one day become an institution where scholars could register for their doctorate programs. Now I know that you will do much more with this, even when I am long gone.

You know I am not a religious person, but I am deeply spiritual. I want to tell you to learn always from those around you—your students and the professors around you will teach you things that you would not otherwise have the opportunity to learn. After I pass away, I pray that you will always be inspired to keep steadfastly on the journey that you have chosen.

Aruna, I wish you boundless happiness. Happiness is often an elusive thing and the quest for it is elusive too, so cultivate the ability to be happy with what you have. Draw your happiness from your family and those who love you for what you are. Happiness is a way of life, it is not anything that you can buy or borrow. Your happiness has to come from within you. Don't let you happiness depend on anyone or anything else.

As you become a leader in your own right, I want to tell

you that a leader should have his or her eyes open at all times, notice things around them, and lead by example. Keep your team happy because they are the people who make you what you are. Your success depends on them. Learn to recognize that often you will know the truth only from the humblest person in your organization because the ones higher up will only want to praise you and your work. Keep in touch with the ordinary folk in your company.

At Finolex, I took joy in interacting with the many people who spent so many decades of their life building our organization. I took great life lessons from the peon in my office who worked for over 39 years for me, so if he wanted to meet me for a mere five minutes, I made sure I met him.

A leader should always be aware of the things around him. Mentor those under you. Don't let the position or the chair that you occupy distract you or make you feel self-important. Always be ready to pitch in with your own hard work. Know everything about your work and your line of business because I truly believe self-help is the best help. I did that when I was building up my small business and grew it to this stage, not with my education but with my common sense and my ability and fierce will to know and understand what goes into the making of every single thing in our group. Aim for that level of knowledge, my dear.

Already, I know that you have embarked on what might seem right now a challenging task of studying for your doctorate. It is a difficult decision to begin late in your life, after your own children are grown up and maybe you are a little afraid, but I will be a very happy father the day you get your doctorate. My lack of a formal education has always been something that I have regretted and I am happy that my daughter is more than making up for this.

I don't have to tell you about hard work and its importance in your life. You work so hard that sometimes I worry you don't give yourself any time to relax and unwind. Hard work remains only a term till you actually do it and I am happy you are working hard. A lot of people speak about God and luck while speaking about their success. Often, these are invisible things and words but you can put meaning into them by doing your work with honesty and commitment. I believe it is possible to create your own luck and find the blessing of God through hard work.

Often, in living our everyday lives, we get carried away so much that we stop noticing our weaknesses. I never went to school and so, I cannot write, don't know my spellings, and it bothers me constantly. Your weakness is the penchant to get much too involved in your work. Learn to delegate. As you grow, it is impossible to keep control of everything yourself. Learn to detach yourself and to stop micromanaging. The body and the soul gets burnt up from too much activity, so learn to rejuvenate by doing something that you like.

Wake up early every day, go for a walk. I have done that every day of my life and I can tell you that there is great merit in working all day and sleeping early. When you wake up early, you experience a freshness of spirit. I believe that when you walk alone in the morning, nature acts as your companion, walking and communicating with you. It is the time of the day that brings fresh ideas, energy,

*and the courage to follow up on doing the things that you
need to do. In the end, I simply want to tell you that I am
immensely proud of you.*

God bless you,
Papa

Renuka Ramnath

At 33, Renuka Ramnath was sitting pretty with a successful career in a reputed bank, an adoring husband, two lovely children, and a picture-perfect life till fate dealt her a cruel card one day that brought her life crashing around her like a pack of cards.

In a minute, a callous truck driver coming down the wrong side of a hairpin bend on a narrow mountain road had crashed his massive vehicle into the car that carried Renuka's happy family on their way back from a precious holiday, snatching away her beloved husband. Suddenly, the man whom she had depended on for everything was no longer around her to lean on, taken away by a cruel twist of destiny.

'Sitting on the embankment, a few feet away from the mangled car in which my husband lay dead, the message came to me from somewhere above that I had to find a way to get over this setback and be back on my feet. Cutting through the noise of my three-year old daughter's frightened wailing, a message came to me that it was now my job to step in and give my children everything that their father would have given them. I would never be able to bring him back but I would do everything humanly possible to make sure that they lacked for nothing else in life.'

Sitting in the cozy comfort of her sprawling farmhouse high up in the smoky blue Western ghats, as the incessant

SUDHA MENON

rain beat on the French windows, Renuka Ramnath poured her heart out, talking about the ups and downs of her life, the things that shaped and made her the woman she is today, the people who held her hands along the way and helped her remain committed to her calling despite a setback that would have paralyzed many ordinary human beings.

There were no commas or full stops in our conversation, and no subject that she shied away from. That is how she lives her life too: no holds barred and no brakes to stop her from getting to her destination. Renuka Ramnath is a woman of extraordinary grit and determination. If you were to box her into a compartment—something she is intensely averse to doing since she does not believe in compartmentalization—she would be in the box on which immensely successful women are labelled 'power woman'. Only a couple of years ago, after spending 23 years at India's second largest private bank as the head of its private equity firm, ICICI Ventures, Renuka quit and decided to chart a different journey, on her own terms. Within months, she was back in business, heading the affairs at MULTIPLES, an equity fund that currently manages $450 million of investors' money put largely on her reputation in the business.

But cut through all the adjectives that describe her name, and the woman who you find underneath is a simple, caring, unbelievably positive woman with a *joie de vivre* that is rare to find in a world that is increasingly like being on a treadmill to nowhere. Meeting her convinced me in many ways that the human mind and its indefatigable spirit can indeed conquer everything that life delivers at our doorstep.

204

When I landed up at her home that morning, my teeth were chattering from the chill of the morning air. I was welcomed in by her aged parents with warmth and care. Her father was busy with his morning prayers while her mother was bustling around in the kitchen, preparing a meal for us. When I finished the interview, I was led into the open kitchen that looked over mountain peaks hidden under dense monsoon clouds, a lazy river snaking its way in the distance, and it all seemed somehow surreal that I should be sitting there eating a simple South Indian meal prepared with love and care by a woman well into her seventies, assisted by her daughter who is a frequent inhabitant of the list of the country's most powerful women.

When you meet them, it is not difficult to imagine where she got her caring nature and her endearing simplicity from. At her current position in life, Renuka can afford a lot of things that money can buy, not just for herself but for her family and her large network of friends. But she has not let it affect her or her children in any way. 'For me, the biggest wealth continues to be the unceasing love of my children, my parents, and my friends scattered all over the world. People are the biggest treasure of my life.'

Renuka writes this simple, heartfelt epistle to her daughter in the faraway upstate New York. She is there and is currently studying Psychology and Education so that she can somehow find a more sensitive way for society to deal with people with mental and emotional disabilities.

Dear Ramya,

I still remember the days when Appa was gone and I used to be frightened about the prospects of bringing up two little children all by myself without his loving presence to guide me along. That seems such a long way ago now and the two of you are sterling young people who make me proud of what you have made out of your lives. People often tell me that I have done a splendid job of raising you as grounded, balanced, and loving children; I know I have and I tell them that I thank God everyday for it as well as all the people who have supported me in doing that.

It is not often that I would write you a letter of this kind but none of what I say here are mere words; they are the stuff that I have experienced in the last fifty years. So it is, in some ways, coming right from the horse's mouth!

Dear Kannamma, you are on the threshold of a life that is brimming with promise and potential and as you set out on a long and fruitful journey, I want to tell you about the things that helped me along the way, when I was like you, a young woman eager to experience a life of her own.

Your grandparents and my siblings—your aunt and uncle and all my cousins—say that even when I was merely three-years-old, I had a mind of my own and refused to let anyone tell me that something was impossible to do. When my grown up siblings and cousins in our large joint family closed the door on my face so that they could learn their music lessons in peace, I banged on the doors everyday and screamed to be let in because I wanted to learn too. My family said it was too early but the endless banging on the door continued till one day the music teacher convinced my parents to let me into the room and I started learning music at that very age of three. Music continues to be one of my biggest passions to this date, a companion that soothes the soul and refreshes the mind when it is restless or fatigued.

That refusal to let other people lay down standards and benchmarks for me has been one of the most important principles of my life and I hope that you can make it yours too.

When I enrolled for a chemical engineering course at the prestigious Veermata Jijabai Technological Institute (VJIT) in 1978, I was only the fourth girl in the institute's 99-year-old history. The Principal of the college did his best to dissuade me, saying I would be alone in a class full of boys and cautioned me that it would be difficult, if I chose that as a profession. He cautioned me that insisting on taking the textile engineering course could possibly mean that I would never get employment because there were not many women tough to handle the heavy textile machinery that I would have to in the industry at that point. My male classmates would often chide me and say that as a woman in that course, I had deprived a deserving male candidate of his seat because I would only finish the course, get married, and bear children. They did not realize that every time they dissuaded me, talked down to me, and demoralized me, I was more determined to show them that I was made of sterner stuff. I thought to myself, 'Just what do they know about me that makes them so sure that I cannot complete this course?'

At each stage in my life, I have set my own internal benchmarks for achieving my personal goals. I have been inspired and motivated by people, but my standards of what constitutes excellence have always been set by me.

Often, my parents and my friends wonder why I am not willing to pause or rest on my laurels and my answer to them is that in my lexicon, the word 'enough' does not exist. For me there is always something that can be improved, something more to be done and learnt, always something more to innovate... It is easy to mistake this as compulsive behavior but I always say that if you enjoy what you do, there is no question of looking at it as a chore. Take joy in doing whatever it is that you want to do and do the best that you can. Kannamma, for me, hard work is the only way to realize God. That, and a deep, unwavering, unfaltering commitment to your chosen path. Get after the thing that you want with single-mindedness, madness even, and that alone will propel you to your destination.

Growing up in a large joint family of very modest means, I was always impressed and touched by the relentless hard work and sacrifices that my elders made so that the entire family got a decent life and good education. My parents never hid their financial struggles from us and we were conscious and grateful for all the things that we got despite our bottom-of-the-middle-class existence. Money was scarce and the elders stretched themselves so that they never had to deny us anything.

Amma would cook for three of us, do her household chores, and stitch frocks for us so that for the price of buying one, we got two dresses each. And, she denied herself even the small pleasure of a single saree in a year, content with the annual gift of one from her brother! My grandmother too was just as hard working and she kept her flock together, making sure that at any special occasion in the house, the entire family from both our mother and father's side partook of the joy. Even today we follow the same practices established by her.

Growing up in that atmosphere made me the person I am today. Seeing their commitment and hard work instilled in me the belief that only academic excellence would give me the opportunities that would somehow help me repay everything they did for us. By the time I was in middle-school, being number one became crazily important for me. And it was also important to me to be number one with a big lead. It seems preposterous now, but that one thing consumed my mind to such an extent that dressing up and wanting to look good in my teenage years was not as important as being the number one in class! Be like that child, let the need to work hard and excel come from within you and you will see that there is no need to compete with any external person or force. When you become your own number one motivator, nothing can stop you from reaching your goals.

When your father went away so unexpectedly, I had no choice but to continue my life without missing a stride because I had the responsibility to look after you and your brother. His death was not the turning point of my life because I had always been highly ambitious, but he was my friend, guide, philosopher, a great father to you, and such a *wonderful companion that I had handed over the charge of everything in our lives to him. It is difficult to imagine now but he was the invisible anchor for our extended family, the guy who organized the kids' education, the family's investment, and the food and entertainment if there was a big family get together. For the eight years of my marriage, I was so immersed in my relationship that I was not even sure whether my career was important or not. I gloriously flirted with the idea that I could have a career while still be a happy housewife who kept a good home, raised kids, and had great family occasions.*

All that changed the day that truck came from the wrong side of the road and crashed into our car, changing the direction of our lives forever. Suddenly I had nobody with who to bounce off an idea, discuss a challenging situation at work with, or ask for help to understand a new concept. He was brilliant but looking back, I think he realized how dependent I was on him. 'I am not the best at everything Renu', he would say. 'Learn to look for the right person for the right thing and you will always get the right feedback and guidance'. I laughed at him then but when he went out of our lives so suddenly, I truly realized the need for self-dependence and the value of reaching out to people.

When he passed away, I had no time to brood, to worry that I was not giving enough attention to my children. Working long hours was not a choice but a need so that I could raise you with all the things that your young lives needed and would need ahead in life. And if I survived the dark periods of grief and the unfairness of life, it was because

I was blessed with a family who stood by me solidly. Your aunt, my sister, is my soul mate, the woman who held my hand through the difficult times, talking to me, staying silent when I needed to look inwards, and intuitively leading me to discover the healing powers of Reiki to soothe my battered soul. My parents stepped into our lives, reassuring me with their kind presence and their support of everything that I did. My father is the rock of my life, someone who has always stood by me, asking no questions. He does not think he has done me a favour by being there for me all through these years, often putting my needs ahead of his. For him, it was the most natural thing to do, an extension of his role as a father. At fifty, I continue to be his little daughter. My brother opened up a new world in my life by literally holding my hand and taking to me our Guru, Sri Sri Muralidhara Swamigal. He has been an emotional anchor and takes so much pride in everything that I achieved. My friends from across the world wrote to me and kept in touch, giving me courage to face the long journey ahead of me. I have got a great deal of support from friends and my extended family, for my early loss, for which I am eternally grateful.

Child, I want you to remember to always cultivate and nurture relationships. In the end, they will be all that matter.

Dear daughter, I learnt early that it is a competitive world out there and nobody will wait around for you to finish dealing with your personal problem before you start performing at work. But even before that, I was driven by a kind of inner calling to put everything in my work. I remember how furious my boss was when I ended up being hospitalized

211

for severe fatigue one day and it was then that my colleagues realized that I was pregnant with my second baby but never told anybody about it because it was a busy period at work. I never wanted to ask for any special treatment to be meted out to me simply because I was a woman.

I don't know if I will do it now but back then, my work was my calling. And it is even now. I truly believe that if you have that one determined goal and pursue it doggedly, everything else will fall in place.

Kanna, learn early on to set your own standards in anything you do as wife, mother, employee, and friend. That is what I did always. People around me never understood what it is that I was chasing when I had already achieved what most of them would not dream of achieving in a lifetime. They never figured out that my driver and benchmark was within myself. Everything that you do should be extraordinary. That might seem like a tall order but that is the only way to do it. In pursuing your goals, be inspired by the ordinary folk who have done unimaginable things just with their passion, creativity, hard work, without the support of networking circles that people from privileged backgrounds enjoy. These are the stories that are lot more encouraging than the inspiration that come from people with privileged backgrounds.

My own mother was a simple village girl who grew up in a highly protected environment but had to come to a big city when she got married. Life was difficult and money was scarce but she managed to look after us with so little resources, feeding everybody who came home.

In some ways, seeing her so, motivated me to take up more responsibilities so that not only could I repay my parents for their sacrifices but also look after you, my children. For several years, your grandfather had to go to work alone in a foreign country so that he could look after his family's needs. It used to hurt me that he was all by himself working hard, cooking on his own, and sending money to us.

So when I threw myself into work with a vengeance after your father died, it was also because I wanted to take care of three generations—my parents, myself, and my children. That was a big motivator for me.

Remember the time we went to your grandfather's village and visited your great aunt who lived there all alone? We arrived there en route to visit the family deity and met this old, poor lady, who had a veritable feast awaiting us when we came back from our prayers. With just her ingenuity and the few humble ingredients she had in her larder, she gave us a memorable meal and when we were ready to leave, she offered us a meal to have on the journey, packed in the only plastic container that she possessed. I hope that you will learn from the spirit of giving that simple lady showed us all those years ago.

I have worked hard to make sure that money does not corrupt our lives. It gives us creature comforts but that has never translated into disregard for either money or human relationships. Your grandfather still tends to the farm while your grandmother still cooks our meals. And I revel in the fact that my children too value the relationships that we have built over the past decades.

Child, I have made more money than we have ever dreamt of in our wildest dreams and yet, it has never been an agenda to chase for us. If you were to ask me what the right thing to do is, I would say it is to make a genuine personal effort to make another person feel loved and wanted. As a young mother who did things for her children, I know that children are a hundred percent more perceptive than we are willing to give them credit for, a thousand times more sensitive than you can imagine, and a thousand times more responsible than we think they are capable of. When you become a mother, show your young ones by example, both by your talk and your actions, what the right things are and they will never do anything that will shame you and themselves.

But that comes much later, doesn't it? As a young woman tiptoeing on the threshold of a promising life of love and fulfillment, you need to know the other secrets that I learnt along the way. There can be no bigger joy than marrying the man you love. But even then, it is important for you not to forget and give up your identity. Women come packaged with generations of conditioning that we have to give ourselves up in the interest of the marriage and our new family.

But I have a secret to tell you. There will be moments of digression when you feel that your only role is being a good wife, mother, and daughter-in-law, but the good part is that you don't really have to forgo one for the other. Don't give up caring for your family, blend into the new family but don't give up your own identity. Don't live with the feeling that you sacrificed your personal goals for your family. Never stop living short of your own full potential, whatever be the compulsion, because if you do that, you will live with that regret all through your life.

There is always a way to find a balance between your home and your career and you alone can decide what that balance is. For me, a large portion of life was my career, then children, then my family, and that left almost no time for myself for almost fifteen years, but I was still happy because that was the balance that I chose for myself! I don't know if you know this but for almost a decade when your brother was growing up into a teenager, we would go to watch his favorite action movies and while he did that, I would catch up on my sleep. When the movie was over, he would wake me up and we would get back home happily.

Kanna, balance to me means: if you have an ambition in life, you should create an environment around you which will give you the unfettered right to go pursue your goal and be totally happy and content in what you are doing. Don't compare your life with that of someone who has other priorities. In life, you are accountable to nobody but yourself. If you live your life being accountable to others, you will end up messing it up and always blaming someone else for the unhappiness it caused you. Saying I am sacrificing for someone else's happiness is a big mistake. Only when you are happy can you make others happy too.

Be happy 365×24×7. Dear Kanna, if you decide today that you want to stay back in the US because your happiness lies there, don't feel pressured to come back home because you feel guilty that I am alone. Only when you are happy can you make me happy, so don't compromise on your needs and happiness. Often a woman is told to blend into the family she marries into. To me, blending into an environment means understanding the value system of the family you are marrying into, respecting it, and complying with it in order to avoid jarring the existing equations in the family. But this should be only to the extent possible when you are in that environment. Remember to always define your own space in your family and to live by what you believe in. Don't change yourself depending on where you end up in marriage.

When I quit ICICI to set up this private equity firm, a lot of people were skeptical; friends and family were concerned about where I was headed, even though their misgivings were out of concern for my well-being.

That venture has now grown to be significant success story and that is because I don't subscribe to any bracketing or boxing of people into categories. I am a great believer of Osho and I believe that boxes are created by people to put others down and put themselves in a position of advantage by getting to live in a less threatened and less competitive world. Likewise, it's with gender.

I truly believe that the only constraints to growth are the ones in the mind. In reality, the world outside is waiting to help you succeed in whatever it is you want to do, if you only reach out to it. If you believe you can do something, pursue it without distraction, without wasting time on fearing failure. Think deeper about how you can get to where you want to. The power of the universe is beyond our imagination and so are its resources. You are the master of your own destiny and nobody else.

As you set out on your own journey, I want to tell you that in life, nothing is more powerful than the power of love. What love can win for you is much more than what your intellect can. Let every engagement of yours be driven by love and genuine interest in people. My first disposition for everybody has always been genuine care and respect for their aspirations and dreams. I know from experience that there is nothing to be gained by being skeptical, over smart, or insecure and these are not crucial to success. Success itself is a nebulous thing. Great things can be achieved with love and by avoiding the dog-eat-dog mentality that seems often to have taken over the environment.

However, all of these things cannot be traded off or practiced to the detriment of competence or performance. If there is an economic activity that you are following, you have to respect that, respect the economic resources that go into it. But that need not be done to the detriment of love and caring. As a teenager, I was thought to be arrogant and opinionated when I was actually only just expressing my conviction about things.

I have learnt to have a complete open-mindedness to others' point of view. I got the gift of positivity from a college mate at VJTI who, besides me, was the only girl in class. When I stood alone in the corridors all those years ago, weeping from the jibes and taunts of my male classmates, she would tap me on the shoulder and tell me to straighten my spine and get back to work. 'If you choose to cry, you will do that for the next twenty years and nobody will care. But if you want to get on with your life and your career, make sure you are accepted by the boys. If you want to be part of the mainstream, figure out what it takes and do that. They are complete without you and you are the one who needs them so you have to make the effort,' she would say. Instead of a cup of tea and a shoulder to cry on, she gave me that sharp wake-up call but it gave me the strength and the confidence to help me through that very difficult period. I can never thank her enough for that lesson well learnt!

There are other things that have been of immense value in my life. Early on in life, I was amazed by the positivity that my grandmother spread around her, by her happiness in the face of great adversity. To this day I can see her going about industriously, creating things out of the little resources she had—shopping bags from old clothes and the floral decorations for the daily puja at home. Our house had lovely things from the stuff that she made out of recycled items because she was an incredibly creative and persevering person. To this day, I don't allow anyone to say anything negative around me. Positivity is contagious, so spread it around. There is nothing that I respect more than creativity and innovation, even if it is something small that the gardener does in our garden. Originality is a rare attribute to be cherished and nurtured. Never let go of your own originality and let society tell you that you are not good enough because you are not like the rest. Each one of us has something unique and it is our duty to preserve that uniqueness.

Remember at all times, my child, to never focus on your

constraints but on your strengths. There will always be someone who will work hard to show you your weaknesses because they gain from it. Nothing is stronger than your own desire to succeed. Sometimes they might do it because they mean you well; use everything as feedback but let your belief in yourself be unshaken, be madly confident about your ability to do something and you will get to your goals. Don't live your life based on other people's expectations or rulings. I followed my own heart and after eighteen years of struggle, it has truly been well worth it.

My dear daughter, collect the goodwill and blessings of your elders. In good times and in times of crisis, that is a priceless treasure to have. So is a certain kind of spirituality, a belief in someone superior to us. When your father passed away, it was my faith in Shrinathji that kept me on my chosen path, pulled me out of the dangers that could have distracted me from my calling. Equally, it was the blessings of my elders, the unending support of my friends that helped me take my life forward.

When my world became a dreary and joyless place after your father's death, it was my belief in God, my guru, and my friends that made it possible for me to remain committed to my purpose. It is my firm belief that the Universe has a role to play in making all of these people come into my life at that point because I was lost and floundering. My sister stepped in, introducing me to the healing powers of Reiki so that I could recover, recharge my energies, and rediscover myself. Since then, I have applied the rejuvenating power of

Reiki at the workplace, introduced my friends and colleagues to it, and have seen everyone benefit from it.

The ability to lead your life with integrity is as important as believing in God. Try to never be obliged to anyone for anything. Don't get into a transaction that puts you in an obligation to anyone because that limits your potential. Every day that you live, live to your fullest potential. That can't be done if you are obliged to someone because both these things are contradictory to each other. If you are obliged to someone, you can't live to your fullest potential without reengaging on your promise to that person. Instead, realize your fullest potential by hard work alone and the power of the Universe will work to make you successful.

It is my refusal to be obliged that makes me want to get out of my bed every morning and do my best. That is what I want for you too, my child.

If I was obliged and I had sold my soul to someone, I would not have the energy to get out of bed each day and do my best. The conflict inside me would have tied me down to my bed, shackled my limbs.

Dear Kannamma, I look forward to seeing you attain the success that you want in the field of your choosing. I am proud that someone as young as you has chosen to follow a calling that is so mature for her age. And I wait for the day when you will use your training in Education and Psychology, to make life more meaningful and joyful for those with psychological and emotional disabilities.

In the end, I want to tell you that at no point of time during my journey have I had a sense of burden for all *the things I have done for my family. I have enjoyed every moment of this tumultuous journey because I have had the blessing of your company. You owe me nothing but your own happiness at all times.*

Love,
Ma

Sanjeev Kapoor

I ndia's culinary maestro, Sanjeev Kapoor, is neither a Michelin-star chef nor has he been hatted—both honours considered to be the highest form of recognition for any chef in the world. In fact, Kapoor makes for the most unlikely chef. He started out in life wanting to be an architect but decided to take up hotel management instead after he failed to make the cut for admissions to the architectural college he had applied to.

That did not, in any way, stop the determined, talented, and perfection-seeking young man from putting every ounce of his soul into his work. Like his father who taught him that knowledge is the key to being the best in your chosen profession, Kapoor has gone about the past few decades learning everything he can about the smallest part of the food business. Kapoor was and continues to be a fearless risk-taker. A few years into his marriage and career as an Executive Chef at a five-star hotel, Kapoor walked away from the job because he felt he was meant for better things in life. What followed was a period of uncertainty before finally landing the television show, Khana Khazaana, the longest-running food show in Asia which turned him into a household name. Homemakers swore by the perfection of his recipes, and where they were earlier usually content with cooking the usual dal, chawal, roti, and subzi, they started experimenting with other forms of food, dishing out pastas, pizzas, fajitas and enchiladas, tapas and tostadas.

Kapoor is the lone ranger who took the path less travelled and discovered the pot of gold at the end of the rainbow. In 2011, he launched FoodFood, his own 24-hour food channel, a feat that only a handful of chefs around the world have been able to pull off. Kapoor's business now includes everything from restaurants and modular kitchens to ready-to-eat meals and kitchen equipment. He writes a letter garnished with love and concern for his two daughters.

Dear Rachita and Kriti,

It has always been my policy not to tell you what to do but to let you learn, instead, from what you see around you. I am hoping you will treat this letter less as a lecture and more as a glimpse into the stuff that has resulted in me becoming the person I am today and the father to two incredibly loving daughters.

If I were to look back over the years and to put my finger on the two or three beliefs that have helped me shape my own destiny, it would be the courage to be different, the willingness to take risks, the ability to have complete belief in yourself and above all, the motivation to work so hard that you become the expert in the space that you have chosen as your calling.

You are young now and on the threshold of a life that will take you along various paths, some smooth, others rough, and many a times the journey will be solitary. But what will come of help to you at such times, as it did for me, is the faith that if you are clear about where you are headed, the way ahead will open up for you. It might take some time but in the end, the path will clear up and you will reach where you always wanted to. The road that will take you to your goal, whatever and wherever it might be, is often not the road that the rest of the world will necessarily trod on, but if you know in your heart that it is the right path for you, take it, nevertheless.

I first realized the importance of standing your own ground at the age of 13, when my father's bank job took us to the capital city of Delhi. My education till then had been at various convent schools across the country where his transferable job took us. And, my stints at these seemingly sophisticated schools had taught me a couple of things about education, including the fact that our schools, sadly, didn't necessarily have the best teachers because our system did not encourage the best students to follow a career in teaching. I knew even at that point that our most important learning comes from the values and the practices that we pick up at home from our parents and elders. It may not qualify as 'structured' education in the conventional sense, but it impacts and influences us so much that there are chances of not forgetting those lessons in our lifetime.

Which is why, in Delhi, I decided that instead of undertaking a long commute to a reputed convent school, I would enroll myself in a government-run school near our *house. My decision surprised my family but I stuck to it, pointing out that the education would be in English and I would also have the luxury of a swimming pool in the campus because this was one of the 'model schools' that the government was setting up. I never used the pool at school ever though!*

Barely had I overcome the first hurdle when I ran headlong into a second, more formidable one. The school offered Sanskrit as an optional language and I decided I wanted to study the language since it would help me score much more than other languages. I had an obsession at that point about being the best in everything I did and scoring well in this language was in line with my strategy. Only, the school refused to allow me to take up that subject because I was the only student who wanted to learn it. When they failed to dissuade me, they summoned my parents and spoke to them about talking me out of it, but I stuck to my guns and simply pointed out that the school had a Sanskrit teacher and it was rule-bound to teach me the language if I wanted to. Eventually they gave in, I got my Sanskrit language training, and went on to score a lot of marks. That one event taught me the lesson that if you believe in something, don't give up or back down just because popular opinion goes against you.

A few years ago, when I first wanted to start my 24-hour food channel, it caused quite a stir because it was something unheard of in India. My friends and colleagues in the industry, heads of other television channels laughed at me saying an ordinary chef had never managed to pull off such an audacious dream anywhere in the world. I would never be able to generate the humungous amount of money that would be required to fund such a project, they warned me. I refused to let the cynicism dampen my spirits and when the large industry heavyweights refused to buy into my idea, I got down to work silently, applying for a license, learning everything that I could about satellite television, the business model, and other technicalities. In the end, I started my own 24-hour food channel, FoodFood, and even if it was delayed—dreams often take time to become reality—I proved that a chef can, in fact, own his own television channel.

Belief has nothing to do with money. With money you may get the arrogance, but it won't make your belief come true. Belief is a state of mind that tells you that you can do it.

My number one rule for my life has been to think differently and go after something that I want, with the belief that I can do it.

If you are willing to take risks, things will work out. Of course, you have to have your basics right and know your subject completely. Most people are bright, intelligent, hard working, but that is not enough. You need to be smart enough to enable yourself to visualize things for a longer term, be different, and then let destiny work its magic.

Prove your expertize and chase your goal till the very end. Starting with no money in my pocket but a bagful of dreams, I now have my own channel. In three years' time, I will spend close to Rs 200 crores on it. The wonderful thing is that not all of this money is my own. The very people who did not believe in me initially are today willing to bet their money on my idea!

Years ago, before I even launched my first book, I launched my recipes on a CD at a time when our computers did not even have CD-ROM drives. My website sanjeevkapoor.com was up and running when large media houses did not have their own websites. My motto even today is to dream big and only then will the dream turn into a reality.

I see so many young, talented people not reach the heights that they could have because they are scared of taking a different path and choose to stick with the old, the tried, and the tested.

When I finished graduation and had to make a career choice, I decided to do a degree in architecture. I was a young, overconfident boy then and only applied for a seat at a nearby college, believing that they would definitely give me a seat. To my horror, I did not cut it in the first attempt and my name was put on the college's waiting list. A close friend then introduced me to the idea of a hotel management degree and even though I had no interest in it—in my head, a chef was a mere cook then and not the glamorous being he is looked as today—I decided to appear for an interview for a lark. To my surprise, I cleared the interview and days later, I got a call from the architecture college as well saying a seat was now available for me there! It was a friend's father who finally helped me decide on following the hotel management degree. 'It is better to excel in a mediocre field than be mediocre in an excellent field,' he told me.

At the end of my three-year course when it was time

for placements for the management training programme at the government-run ITDC hotel, the selection panel suggested that I follow a career in kitchen management instead of absorbing me for a hotel management placement. I was furious and accused them of discriminating against me because I came without 'connections'. The senior most member of the selection panel managed to convince me that I would have a place in hotel management if I so wanted. He told me that I was very good with the kitchen and food side of the business and told me to go home and think about it before I made my choice. By the time I went back to him the next day, my mind was clear and I had decided to take his suggestion and adopt the kitchen and food space as my career. Looking back, I like to think that I made the right decision. I truly believe that if you have the guts to stand out in a crowd, the chances of your standing out in life are much higher.

Kriti, you have your mind set on being a professional runner and have been following that passion for years now. Sometimes I am worried about you because this is a career that will be fraught with hurdles, one in which the chances of success are way limited than other spheres, simply because of the way sports is perceived in our country. But having followed my own dreams without heeding popular opinion and without always looking at the practical side of things, I want you to pursue your dream till the very end. Become the best runner that this country has produced.

Years ago, when I quit my job as Executive Chef at the Centaur hotel in Mumbai, your mother and I had no house of our own and had less than a lakh between us. But I quit because I was convinced I was meant for better things in life. I was working for nearly eighteen hours a day and was getting nowhere fast. I was looking at master chefs who had taken twenty years of slogging to get to that post and I was determined to not go down that route. Luckily , my tryst with television took off around that time and that too because I managed to convince the bosses at Zee TV that their food show would have much more potential if they called it 'Khana Khazana' instead of 'Sreeman Baawarchi.' I used my management education and my marketing skills to convince them and by the end of it, they were so sold on my idea and my ease with television as a medium, that I became the face of the by-now longest-running food program on television in India. What worked for me is the fact that I was a good teacher and I decided to use the show to teach viewers what they wanted to know instead of simply having me show off my skills. If they failed in their kitchen with my recipes, I would fail too and so I began with simple recipes such as the humble lassi that would make them succeed. That simple formula clicked and made me a household name in Indian homes and ever since then, my strategy has been to never set up my team for failure by giving them responsibilities that they are not equipped to handle.

My dear Rachita, my father taught me the value of knowledge. He was a banker and he spent the better part of his day at work but he continuously surprised us with the span of his knowledge on everything. He was on the lending side of the business and would say that if he did not know *everything about the borrower's business, his bank would run the risk of losing its money. When you study something, make that a journey of learning. If you are not learning while studying, it is simply a waste of time.*

Another thing that he used to say was that good things happen only to people who believe good things can happen to them. I have trained myself to notice only the good things in life, the positives in people. I try and surround myself with positive people and learn from them continuously. My parents also taught us to maintain equilibrium in our lives. 'Don't revel too much in your joy or drown yourself too much in your sorrow. Strike a balance,' they would say.

Remember how you used to be scared and worried about your math exams? I told you it was perfectly okay even you scored a zero in the test and that one thing liberated you from your fear forever. There is a learning there for all of us. Fear of failure keeps people from trying to do anything that is out of their comfort zone.

Remember always that the values your parents instill in you are always something you should follow. Parents are the only people in your life who have no ulterior agenda other than your well-being on their minds.

The other things that have also made a difference in my life include the ability to challenge myself continuously, think ahead, and plan for the long-term. 'Always keep the big picture in mind when you plan your life', my father would say. To add to that, I want to tell you that it is also necessary to do many things right consistently and take an informed, long-term view of things. You may take a path that you have *not taken before but there have been lots of visionaries before you, who have spent their lifetimes making that road for you. In comparison your contribution is nothing, so keep that in mind as you move forward.*

I want you to know that as both of you grow up to become young, independent women with your own individual dreams and aspirations, restless to follow your own path, all I wish for you is happiness. But the definition of that happiness should be yours alone.

Relationships are extremely important for a happy life, children, so remember to build and nurture them and to have trust and faith in them. Skepticism and cynicism are the death knell of relationships.

Sometimes, I feel like telling you things about life so that I can save you the pain that comes from making mistakes. But I don't think preaching helps. Live your life like you would peel an onion, each layer at a time, enjoying and savouring each moment, so that life becomes your biggest teacher. There is great merit in learning things on your own instead of having your parents tell you stuff because, if everything is revealed in advance, it is like watching a movie beginning with the end!

Sometimes people ask me what is the meaning of success. To me, success is equal to happiness. Success does not drive me, happiness does.

The birth of my daughters was my biggest happiness for a long time. Till my father passed away, I did not know what my greatest sorrow was. Today, when I get the time to call my mom twice a day and chat with her, that gives me immense happiness, contributing to other people's happiness by helping them get a job, teaching them a skill or just giving them my time gives me happiness. Sometimes at home on a Sunday, I find happiness by just polishing my furniture so that it shines.

Be flexible with your thoughts and attitude and be sensitive to the people around you. In relationships and business, be fair. You can't build businesses treading on other people's lives. When I started my first restaurant in Dubai thirteen years ago, I had a relationship with the family of my then franchisee. Just three years after the restaurant opened, he passed away unexpectedly. But the family needed the money and so, despite the fact that the restaurant was being run by someone else, I still continue to give them a percentage of my royalty from that restaurant.

There are other things too which I hope you can avoid doing. I don't suffer fools and expect perfection from myself and others around me. But I have started changing that now because that is too high a standard for most people. I want to tell you that it's okay to make mistakes so long as you accept your mistake and make amends.

Respect the people around you. Respect as a value is something that has to be cherished. Respect your resources too. Wealth is not a value; spending with prudence is, and I am happy to see both of you have picked up our attitude about wealth.

I remember how upset you were a couple of years ago when I came to school in my new BMW to pick you up. You were aware that not all the students in school had the

*privileges that you did and you did not want to be insensitive
to their feelings. It made me proud when you expressed that
thought to me.*

*In the end, I want the both of you to remember that if
anytime you want to come to me for a solution or want your
mother or me to just listen to you, we are always there, no
matter how busy we are. We love you.*

Papa

Shaheen Mistri

Shaheen Mistri's life changed in a few seconds one summer 23 years ago when the 18-year-old American resident was waiting at a traffic signal in a car that would take her to her grandparents' plush home in South Mumbai. It was then that a group of street urchins surrounded the car, pressing their noses into the windows, begging, demanding some money so they could quell the hunger pangs that drove them crazy. The privileged daughter of a senior banker never could forget the image of those grubby children, their eyes full of hope but doomed to a life of begging, because they did not have the gift of education.

The young woman never went back to the US where she was studying but made the slums of Mumbai her home, working relentlessly to bridge the inequities in Indian society by educating its children. Her hard work paid off when Akanksha, the first organization that she set up for underprivileged children, caught the imagination and had young volunteers lining up to help her out. Akanksha touches the lives of over 4000 children through 40 centers and 13 schools in Mumbai and Pune, which delivers not just quality education but life skills that boost their self-esteem and empower them with income generating abilities.

Seventeen years after she started Akanksha, Shaheen took another leap of faith when she started Teach For India, an

SUDHA MENON

audacious venture that ropes in outstanding young graduates and professionals to dedicate two years of their life to teach in low-income schools for two years. The Fellowship enables them to become lifelong leaders advocating for educational equity.

Shaheen's daughters have grown up living their mother's dream, accompanying her mother as she visits the poorest communities in Indian cities, playing with the children of those communities and developing sensitivity to the inequities that are the scourge of Indian society.

Here she writes a simple poem to her children that underlines the strength of her own belief and her bonding with them.

Dear Samara and Sana,

If I could give you anything
I'd show you the times when I was really myself
When I did what I believed in
When I followed my heart
When I tried to live my potential.

And most important,
I'd show you some of what I wonder for you.

I wonder how to
Show you fun

240

That fun is fun
For everyone

To always take
The time to see
The bubble floating
Color-free

I wonder how to
Show you fair
That all things need
The greatest care

To push you hard
And gently too
To strive for greatness
In what you do

I wonder how to
Teach you right
And keep you safe
And hold you tight

And set you free
But not so free
And let you be
What you can be

Love you,
Mama

Zia Mody

I arrived for my 6.30 pm meeting with Zia Mody, possibly India's best-known corporate dealmaker and legal eagle, expecting that she was going to be at the end of her working day and relaxed for a long chat with me. I was mistaken.

I was ushered into the conference room of her 23rd floor office in one of Mumbai's high-rise buildings, just a stone's throw away from the famed Queen's Necklace, and was treated to coffee and biscuits before she bustled in, a smiling bundle of energy that seemed difficult to contain in the room. She looked like everybody's friendly neighborhood aunt, the one you slink off to for some tender loving care when your mother has put you in the dog house for some nameless misdemeanor. But those who have mistaken her for that have discovered in the past that it was a completely wrong and very expensive error.

When Zia, a student of Cambridge and Harvard Law School, decided to start her own litigation practice, she ran into a glass wall straight away with many a client rolling their eyes in disbelief that a woman would handle their case. She had two burdens to bear—that of being a woman in a completely male-dominated space and that of being the daughter of India's former attorney general and brilliant legal mind, Soli Sorabjee. Zia was vexed and she turned to her mother for advice. She got sound advice from the mother who told her to ignore the whispers and get down to the business of proving that she could become a career attorney who could beat not just her father but any man in the same business.

In the following decades, Zia's firm AZB & Partners has become one of the most sought after in the legal space, known for sorting out the most complex corporate disputes and closing several expensive and prestigious acquisitions for some of the country's top corporate houses, including Tata Steel's high profile acquisition of UK steel-maker Corus, in a jaw-dropping $12 billion deal. The firm followed this up with advising the Aditya Birla group during its $6 billion plus acquisition of Atlantis-based aluminum maker Novelis and later, Tata's takeover of Jaguar Land Rover.

My meeting with Zia was interrupted several times when she had to retreat into her office to attend conference calls. She told me later that she preferred coming into office after sunset in order to be able to work more efficiently in the still of the night, without distractions, before heading back home after sometimes having put in over fifteen hours at work!

When she is not working at the frantic pace that she goes by, Zia is a practicing member of the Baha'i faith and doting mother to three daughters with whom she does not get to spend the time that her mother spent in raising her. Her mother, she recalled fondly, spent her days teaching her not just sewing, embroidery, dancing, and music but also taught her about the importance of the woman being a unifying element in her family and in the community. Zia did try to ape her mother and teach her children some of the skills that she has but eventually gave up when her own career gathered steam. Which is why, she cherishes the couple of family vacations that she takes every year with her childhood crush and now husband Jaydev and their three daughters.

In this touching letter to her daughters, Zia tells them about the importance of doing whatever it is they do, with passion, being grateful for the generosity of God in their lives, and being happy in all circumstances or with whatever choices that have made.

❧

My dearest Anjali, Aarti, and Aditi,

It seems like only yesterday that you came into my life, each one of you so cherished, so much loved and doted upon by Pa and me, and each one of you adding richness and color into our lives. I don't know if I ever told you this but Pa loved children so much that he almost wanted me to get pregnant the day after we got married! I completely resisted.

It has been a long journey for all of us and it seems almost unbelievable at times to see all three of you grown up into young women now with your lives charted before you.

Now that we have put all the birthday parties, magicians, pink frocks, and late night ice-cream treats behind us, I would love to get you together to tell you a few things that I know that you are already aware of, but are still worth saying.

SUDHA MENON

The other day somebody asked me what I think are the most important things for our daughters to know, as they set out on the journey of their own lives. These are the few things that I always want to convey to my daughters, and I think holds true for any mom in general.

As clichéd as it sounds, my princesses, what I want most for you is to learn to live your life with great self-respect and dignity. That is the most important thing of all for a woman, anywhere in the world. That and to do something the three of you love to do. Often my friends, and sometimes you three too, wonder where I get all my energy from and how I manage to stay awake at nights so that I get work done at the office, late into the night when the world is fast asleep. My reply, always, is very simple. I am in love with what I do and that alone is enough to give you all the energy you need. That, plus being happy and being grateful for the generosity of God in your lives. Happiness gives you a kind of energy boost that nothing else can give, so cultivate the ability to be happy in whatever circumstances or choices that you have made.

My most fervent prayer to God, the one prayer that I hope He is listening to, is that my daughters remain grounded in their faith to him. My dears, I can't tell you enough about the importance of faith in our lives. When everything in our lives seem to have gone horribly wrong or topsy turvy, faith alone has the strength to keep us moving forward. I hope always that you will believe in the Almighty and His creation and that you fear and love God in equal measure.

Retribution by God is a good thing to fear, it keeps all of us on the straight and narrow, you know.

I often get the feeling that young people don't think they will ever die and so they don't start building their life's balance sheet till much later. My belief in the Baha'i faith has helped me personally withstand a lot of very challenging times and you know how much I try to impart that faith to all you sisters. There are times that I wish and hope that you discover the power of prayer because I sometimes worry that you need to have enough faith. I want to tell you today that the connection with God is something that will help weather a lot of storms in life and believe me, there are going to be many of those.

This means having the inner conviction that there is a superior force more powerful than us human beings, a conviction that every test that comes your way is yours for you to conquer for Him. I get nervous sometimes for you, my children. I worry that God has been kind to us and things have been so smooth that I wonder how my princesses will deliver when God finally tests them with struggles and hardships.

Like every parent of daughters, I too worry about your future, pray that you find wonderful partners who will love, cherish, and respect you for what you are. I got married to my childhood sweetheart and so the path of an arranged marriage for you has never struck your parents. In some ways, I know you will find the right companions because we have inculcated the right values in you, opened up your minds by making sure you have travelled all over the world, been exposed to different cultures and people, and know to hold your own in most circumstances.

Marriage, children, and life will happen to you but through all that, I want to urge all three of you to go find your individual place in the sun.

Anjali (Anjoss), I can't believe that my first-born, the little girl for who we prepared a nursery with so much enthusiasm months before her arrival, has now travelled around the world, and has found her own groove in designing furniture. We should have seen that coming because even as a child, you amazed us with your love for stylish clothes, your eye for detail, and your insistence that everything around you had to be 'just so'. At the same time, you juggle your commitment to your NGO and pack your day completely. Sometimes I see you looking tired but think this is your time for hard work. This is your beginning.

Aarti (Artuss), my second born, you have no idea how much I am waiting for you to finally discover that law is truly your calling. I'm hoping that the three years that you will spend in New York for your law degree will convince you that there is merit in what your mother is doing. I pray sometimes that you will join me in my profession but if you discover something else that engages you more than law, I'm still going to be happy for you.

Aditi (Aduben), my youngest, your father is convinced you are our brightest daughter, the one who will outperform her siblings, once you discover what it is that your heart desires. So you have to live up to our highest expectations!

While I am confident all of you are perfectly able to manage your lives on your own, there are things that I want to tell you anyways, things that I learnt from my own parents.

Someday, whenever you find your life partner, remember to go join his family as a happy agent who nurtures them and not as a divisive wife. Make his family yours in every way possible. My mother used to tell me before I got married to your father, that I was actually marrying my mother-in-law. Now that might seem funny to you but don't forget that it is that lady who has made your future life partner the splendid person that you love, so gain her confidence first, make her your friend, and that is a surefire way to a happy life. My mom told me to accept the fact that there were people in your partner's life before you came along and there will be no cause for whining and complaining after marriage. Don't worry about the petty and the inconsequential, fight the big battles of life, not the small ones. Ignore them and they will cease to seem so important.

When your kids come along, don't forget to teach them the values that your parents inculcated in you and it is my belief that they will be able to lead richer, more fulfilled lives from that.

It is also important for a woman to have a career of her own, something that fulfills her intellectual needs and keeps her independent financially. My philosophy about this is to build up your career and a dignified one at that, one step at a time, without faltering. There will be moments when things overwhelm you but stick to your chosen path. When you work, give it your all, don't be lazy about it or take it for granted. There is no point in being casual.

Very often I tell you that nothing is worth losing your sleep over or falling from grace in your own eyes. Don't, knowingly, take decisions that will affect your reputation, hurt your conscience, or prevent you from sleeping peacefully at night. Moral decisions that affect these three things are simply not worth it. A lie always gets caught and it looks bad when it does. There is no upside to a lie. If the truth had come out for the first time, it would not have been a great deal and I think that there is nothing that a 'sorry' cannot fix. Take the path of truth as much as possible and when you mess up, learn to say 'sorry' too. It helps. And when things seem to get out of control and you need a shoulder to rest your burden on, be secure in the knowledge that we are always there to take your side, comfort you and support you as you fight your battles. Again, remember: fight only the big battles not the small, inconsequential ones. Be strategic!

One of the things our parents taught us as kids is that wealth is transitory and that creating our own wealth is a better option than inheriting it. And as young adults, we always believed our parents should utilize their wealth the way they please because we would give it away anyways. God has always been very kind to us siblings: material wealth has always been there but we have grown up with a sense that there is only so much we can eat. I believe that the more we give away with a higher level of pain, the more we will get because God does not like to be in our debt. His will is to never be in our debt and so He will make sure you have plenty. If you have the faith enough to give away without the expectation of anything in return, you will never want anything in life. In my life this has been proven.

I firmly believe that beyond a point money should not be the main reason for things that we do in life. Not all of us can completely sacrifice our lives for the good of society but each of us can partake in many small acts that helps the community around us. What matters is to do what is in our capacity to do, gain the respect, love, and adoration of the people around us, and then leverage your reputation to help society in a larger, more meaningful way. Anjali, you have no idea how much it delights me when you already show signs of having a generous attitude at such a young age. Your work with NGOs, particularly the project where you tried to use solar lanterns that will eventually bring light to underprivileged families, filled me with pride. As we get older, working for a cause that is beyond and larger than our own livelihood concerns should be a significant part of our lives.

In a way, Papa and I are confident the value system that we have inculcated has already given you a firm footing and a healthy respect for what the community will expect from you. You all have come a long way from the time your father once pointed to the fridge at home and asked Aditi how much she thought it cost. Her answers ranged from Rs 50 to Rs 1 lakh. That was many years ago. Now we are confident each of you have a much better understanding of ground realities.

What I am about to say will sound surprising, but let me say it anyways. Nothing can substitute the power of bonding between all five of us as a family. I know I haven't spent enough of that time. Very often, in our fast-paced lives, we overlook this simple truth and come to regret it later on. As parents we had resolved to do at least a couple of shared vacations every year, when we get to hang out together, just having fun and sharing the stuff that is going on in our lives. I'm hoping that when your children come along, you will do the same with them.

As a young girl there were times when I would resent all the stuff that my Nanima would make me do. She insisted I do everything—learn piano, Indian dancing, cooking classes, horse riding, sewing… I occasionally resented it but in retrospect, all those things shaped the person I am today. I benefitted from each of the things that I learnt as a child. I tried to do that for you kids too, piano, tabla, dancing, riding class, and indulged your fancy for ballet. So there it is, my Anjoss, Artuss and Aduben, I could not do as much as my own mother could do for me because I was a working mother but I made sure that you are never going to regret that you did not get an opportunity to learn something that would have enriched your lives.

Every moment that we spend with you is such a precious gift. We soak up the affection that you give us so generously. All the BBM's we get from you and all the phone calls Aarti makes from New York are wonderfully precious. I have saved many. Even some angry ones! Sometimes, when I worry that I don't spend enough time with my children, I am blessed by the fact Pa can't have enough of each of you everyday. He has been the rock for all four of us with his continued presence in our everyday lives. And someday I hope that when you become mothers, you will remember to do all the things that your grandmother and your mother did for their children. Give them the gift of your time when they need it. More than I could do.

In a chaotic, often unpredictable world, it gives me joy to know that you are incredibly positive, forward-looking, loving, and kind children. These are gifts that will always help you.

In the end, I want to tell you about a very special secret to a happy life: My grandmother and my mother gave me as their legacy an intense sense of internal pride. I want to add to that and tell you to cultivate the consistent ability to look upon someone as a mentor or role model, a person who you will not just learn from but also derive comfort and faith that will stand by you during tough times.

My grandmother was a feisty, tough woman, full of beans and boy oh boy, she was a deliverer! She travelled all over the world, had five kids, lived her life with unstoppable enthusiasm and energy, and had complete conviction that her faith would see her and family through life. She was my hero and she left a lasting impression on my life. That is what I want you all to remember. Leave a lasting impression on your family.

I love you all completely,
Mom

ACKNOWLEDGEMENTS

This book would never have been written without the unstinting support of my loving family and friends. You stood by me resolutely in what has been a watershed year in my life, providing me a non-judgemental space for my endless griping about life in general, your shoulders to cry on, great amounts of ginger tea to pick me up, not to forget the love, laughter, and huge amounts of encouragement for everything that I have dared to undertake. I owe you all, big time.

This book wouldn't be what it is without the generosity of all the people who have written letters in it to their precious children. They set aside their invaluable time to share the highs and lows of their lives with me. I am grateful for their time and patience and thank them for allowing me a peek into their lives when they were in the early stages of becoming today's trendsetting leaders. Sharing their lives, even if it was for a little while, changed me in many sorts of ways.

This book would not be if it were not for Milee Ashwarya who picked up my precious baby and nurtured it as if it were her own. Milee shared my excitement, motivated me with her continuous admiration for my work, and egged me to push myself beyond what I thought I was capable of. Thank you, Gurveen Chadha, for editing my book, much like a fond mother who will only send her child to the party after making sure she is well-groomed and dressed up.

This book would never be complete without the loving presence of my precious daughter, Nayantara. Each day that I live, I strive to do the best I can in everything that I do so that she will learn by example from her mother.

I would also like thank the scores of other people who helped me in putting this together—enthusiastic and diligent assistants, to the men and women who have written in this book, and my own staff, who treated this as their project and made the road smooth and hassle-free for me.

A Note on the Author

Sudha Menon is the author of four bestselling non-fiction books: *Devi, Diva or She-devil: The Smart Career Woman's Survival Guide*, *Leading Ladies: Women Who Inspire India*, *Legacy* and *Gifted*. A former newspaper journalist, Sudha is now a columnist, a writing coach and a speaker on diversity and inclusion issues. Her books have been translated into Marathi, Hindi and Kannada.

Sudha recently launched Writing with Women, a series of workshops to encourage women from diverse backgrounds to share their experiences through the written word.

She is also the founder of both Get Writing, a workshop that mentors aspiring writers, and Writing in the Park, an initiative to get people to explore their creativity in the outdoors, penning their stories in public parks and gardens.

Capt. Gopinath with his family

Capt. Gopinath at the wedding of his elder daughter Pallavi

Krith and Pallavi with their parents

Anjali with her father Deep Anand in London at her Graduation Ceremony

K.V. Kamath's daughter Ajnya decided to put her career on hold to raise her children in the United States

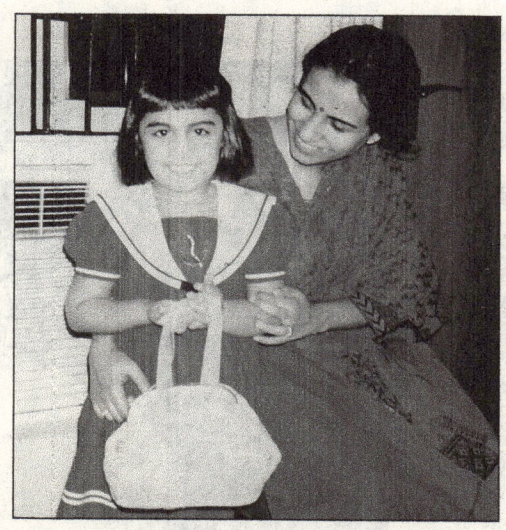

Chanda Kochhar's absence from home for long hours at work made her daughter Aarti an independent soul, who often became the mother-figure for her younger brother

Following her parent's footsteps, Amit Chandra's daughter Anna is sensitive to the fact that the world is a very unequal place. She is comfortable sharing her privileges with those less privileged

Amit enjoys the company of his daughter who came late into their life

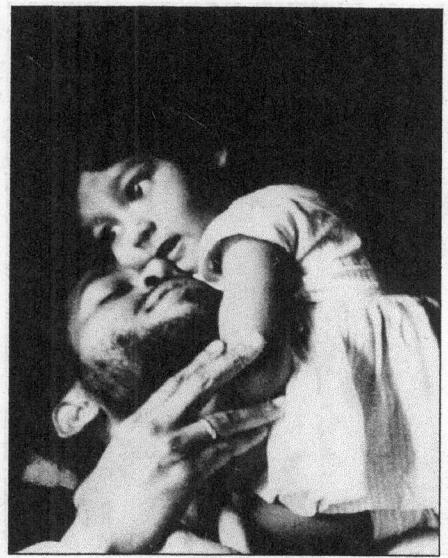

Nandita with her Baba

For many years Nandita Das believed that fathers were supposed to stay at home and look after the home and children while mothers went to work. He was and is her constant companion in the journey of life

Former badminton ace Prakash Padukone says his family always knew that daughter Deepika was born for showbiz. This picture of Deepika as a little girl says it all

Deepika with her parents

Ganesh Natarajan with his daughter Karuna

Ganesh Natarajan grew up as a God-fearing boy but lately, his scientist daughter Karuna and their lively debates have made him agnostic

Kishore Biyani is more of a friend than a father to his two daughters, Ashni and Avni

Like mother, like daughter. Mallika and Anahita take their message of peace, equality, and gender-sensitivity to people through the medium of dance and drama

Ajay Piramal draws inspiration from the Bhagavad Gita. He tells daughter Nandini that faith and compassion can go a long way in making us better people

Infosys Co-founder Narayana Murthy revelled in the company of his children and spent happy evenings telling them stories of their ancestors

Pradeep Bhargava with his daughter Pooja

Your employers can do without you but you are indispensable to your family. A close brush with mortality woke Bhargava up to this fact. Sharing some time with Pooja in this picture

P. P. Chhabria always regretted not completing his education. Today, he is proud that daughter Aruna steers the higher education institute, set up by him

Shaheen with her two daughters who share their mother's vision of an equal world in which every child gets quality education

*Live your life with dignity and fulfil yourself with meaningful work.
Zia Mody shares a joyous moment with her three daughters*

Zia with her two daughters

Dream big and work hard to get to your goal, says Sanjeev Kapoor. Each child should be free to decide the course of their own life and also be taught the importance of hard work and self-belief early in life.

Chef Sanjeev with daughters Rachita and Kriti

Chef Sanjeev Kapoor spending time with his daughters Rachita and Kriti

Become the most positive person you know; live each day like it is your last day on earth; love and respect your family and friends, and have faith in God—Renuka Ramnath shares her secret to a happy life with daughter Ramnya

Renuka with her daughter Ramya

Renuka on holiday with her daughter Ramya